# Reflections on the Social Thought of Allama M. T. Jafari

## Rediscovering the Sociological Relevance of the Primordial School of Social Theory

Seyed Javad Miri

UNIVERSITY PRESS OF AMERICA, ® INC.
*Lanham • Boulder • New York • Toronto • Plymouth, UK*

Library of Congress Control Number: 2010927671
ISBN: 978-0-7618-5191-2 (paperback : alk. paper)
eISBN: 978-0-7618-5192-9

# Contents

# Foreword

It is an honour, indeed, to have been invited by Dr. Seyed Javad Miri to write this foreword for his new study on Allama Mohammad Taqi (Taghi) Jafari (known as Allama Jafari). I am very glad that this study on Allama Jafari's contributions to Muslim Enlightenment now appears in print. Being a liberal Catholic, an Austrian, and an empirical world systems researcher, I will concentrate here on some aspects that might be especially important to the Muslim readership of this study.

As early as 1674, Vienna University had already begun to teach Oriental languages, and in 1754, the Oriental Academy, a kind of state think-tank on "Oriental questions," was founded. Further milestones in the path of peaceful coexistence of the world religions in Europe emanating from Austria were the "AustrianToleranzpatent" (*Edict of Tolerance*) of 1781–82 and the "Staatsgrundgesetz" (*Basic law on the general rights of citizens*) of 1867. In 1912, a law was passed providing recognition of the adherents of Islam according to the Hanafite rite as a religious community,[1] which was a further milestone of Western tolerance *vis-à-vis* Islam, for it was the first time that a major Western country had recognized Muslims as an official religious group.

Vienna was also the city of the global humanist and Muslim convert Dr. Baron Omar Rolf von Ehrenfels (1901–1980), who accepted Islam in 1927. He was an Austrian anthropologist and Orientalist who became a refugee from the Nazi terror in 1938 when he fled to India for asylum. In India, he became a leading researcher on Islam and an early champion of Muslim feminism. Only now is the importance of his theories being properly appreciated. In my view, further studies could highlight the parallels between the theological and sociological thought of Allama Jafari and Omar Rolf von Ehrenfels.

Last, but not least, Vienna before 1938 had its own Sephardic synagogue, which was called *Turkish Temple*. Built in 1887, it was destroyed during the November 1938 pogrom by Nazi mobs. The Viennese Sephardic community was founded in 1736 by descendants of Jews who had been expelled from Spain centuries before and who had found asylum in Turkey under Sultan Bāyezīd II. These Jews had maintained their customs and language (*Djudeo-Espanyol*) and the pleasant memories of Turkish tolerance and hospitality during all those centuries. Their story, which ended in the pogroms in Germany and Austria, is a stark reminder of the fact that Europe cannot always claim to be associated with tolerance, nor can it seriously associate Islam with intolerance. In this regard, it is also pertinent to recall Behiç Erkin (1876–1961), a Turkish army officer, the first director of the Turkish State Railways, Minister of Public Works, diplomat, and co-founder of the Turkish intelligence service *Milli Emniyet Hizmeti*, who, during his tenure as Turkish Ambassador to Paris from 1939 to 1943, saved some 20,000 Jewish lives from the Holocaust by providing them with Turkish passports and organizing twenty trains so that they could flee to Turkey.

Dr. Javad Miri's exploration of the fascinating depths of Allama Mohammad Taqi Jafari's thoughts about Muslim Enlightenment and the foundations of the social sciences alert me in a positive way. Such philosophical studies are very necessary and must be linked in a way to recent empirical surveys about Muslim receptivity to democracy. One of the hardest tasks in the fight against global terrorism will be to convince Muslims worldwide that not "Jews" but, rather, dictatorships are their enemy. The global existence of what could be called "Muslim Calvinist attitudes," as reflected in the findings of my most recent publication (Tausch, 2009), is a sign of hope; and works like this book by Dr. Miri will, I hope, contribute to ongoing Muslim debates about contemporary challenges.

Defending the values of enlightenment and rationalism and pursuing dialogue between the major global civilizations will be an important task at the global level in years ahead, and with respect to this, the present new book by Dr. Miri acquires particular importance for students of global politics and political thought.

Let me quote here Omar Rolf von Ehrenfels:

The essential features of Islam, which impressed me most and attracted me to this great religion are as follows:
1. The Islamic teaching of successive revelation implies in my opinion the following: The source from which all the great world religions sprang is one. The founders of these great paths, prepared for peace-seeking mankind, gave witness to one and the same basic divine teaching. Acceptance of one of these paths means search for Truth in Love.

2. Islam, in essence, means peace in submission to the Eternal Law.
3. Islam is, historically speaking, the last founded among the great world religions on this planet.
4. Prophet Muhammad is the messenger of Islam and is thus the last in the sequence of great religious world-prophets.
5. The acceptance of Islam and the path of the Muslims by a member of an older religion thus means as little rejection of his former religion as, for instance, the acceptance of Buddha's teachings meant the rejection of Hinduism to the Indian co-nationals of Buddha. It was only later that schools of thought within Hinduism rejected the Buddhist way as heretical. The differences of religions are man-made. The unity is divine. The teachings of the Holy Qur'an stress this basic unity. To witness it means acceptance of a spiritual fact, which is common to all men and women.
6. The spirit of human brotherhood under the all-encompassing divine fatherhood is much stressed in Islam and not hampered by concepts of racialism or sectarianism, be it of linguistic, historic-traditionalistic, or even dogmatic nature.
7. This concept of divine fatherly love, however, includes also the motherly aspect of Divine love, as the two principal epithets of God indicate Al-Rahman and Al-Rahim, both being derived from the Arabic root *rhm*. The symbolic meaning of this root equals Goethe's *Das Ewing-Weibliche Zieht uns hinan*, whilst its primary meaning is womb.

[...] In this spirit the prophet gave these unforgettable words to his followers: "Paradise lies at the feet of the Mother."[2]

Basically, then, such a perspective is similar to that of the American sociologist Amitai Etzioni, who stated the following:

Islam is no different than the other major religions. For every Muslim who favors a religious war, there are many who see jihad as a spiritual journey of self-improvement. For every Muslim who blindly accepts [...] rulings [...], there are many more who favor communal consultation—the notion of *shura*. Hence, rather than vainly trying to replace religious education with secular teaching, the issue should be what kind of religious education is made available.

Teaching Western, secular ethics, such as the moral theories of Immanuel Kant and John Rawls, will not get one much traction in large parts of the devout Muslim world. Instead, the best remedy to extremist, violence-prone interpretations of Islam is a moderate, albeit religious, one. Muslims accept that while there is the text of the Qur'an, there are also records of the words and deeds of the Prophet known as hadith. These different texts open the door to varying interpretations of Islam rather than simply going "by the book," tolerating only one strict and rigid interpretation. This is especially true about the status of women, which is much less restricted in some texts than in others. Also, moderates hold that although there are three major "Abrahamic" religions, in which, respectively, Muhammad, Christ, and Moses play a key role, all are to be respected as those of "People of the Book."

In the United States, we hear a largely liberal chorus arguing that valued education should take place only at home. However, given the beleaguered state of the family in much of the modern world—and the cacophony of commercial and sexual voices that youngsters are increasingly exposed to—schools should play a role in the proper upbringing of the next generation. Religion is the major source of such education, especially in large parts of the Muslim world. It follows that the choice the United States and its allies often face—to the extent that they are involved in reforming Muslims schools in the first place—is not between Islamic or secular education, but rather between Islamist and moderate religious education."[3]

It is in this sense that I warmly welcome the publication of this work by Dr. Seyed Javad Miri.

Vienna and Leopoldsdorf, near Vienna
Arno Tausch,[4] August 2009
Adjunct Professor of Political Science
University of Innsbruck, Austria

## LITERATURE AND FURTHER SUGGESTED READINGS TO APPRECIATE THE IMPORTANCE OF DR. SEYED JAVAD MIRI'S STUDY

Amin, S. 1994. *Re-reading the Postwar Period: An Intellectual Itinerary.* Translated by Michael Wolfers. New York: Monthly Review Press.

Armstrong, K. 1992. *Muhammad: A Biography of the Prophet.* San Francisco: Harper SanFrancisco.

———. 1993. *A History of God: The 4000-Year Quest of Judaism, Christianity, and Islam.* New York: A.A. Knopf. Distributed by Random House.

———. 2000. *Islam: A Short History.* New York: Modern Library.

———. 2006. *Muhammad: A Prophet for Our Time.* New York: Atlas Books/Harper Collins.

Arrighi, G. 1995. *The Long Twentieth Century. Money, Power and the Origins of Our Times.* London, New York: Verso.

Balic, S. 2001. *Islam für Europa: Neue Perspektiven einer alten Religion.* Köln and Vienna: Böhlau.

Bardakoglu, A. 2006. *Religion and Society: New Perspectives from Turkey.* Ankara: Turkish Presidency of Religious Affairs.

Barro, R. J. 2004. "Spirit of Capitalism Religion And Economic Development." *Harvard International Review* 25(4): 64–67.

Etzioni, A. 1968. *The Active Society: A Theory of Societal and Political Processes.* London: Collier-Macmillan. New York: Free Press.

———. 1996. *The New Golden Rule: Community and Morality in a Democratic Society.* New York: Basic Books.

Hermann, P., and A. Tausch, eds. 2005. *Dar al-Islam: The Mediterranean, the World and the Wider Europe. Vol. 1. The "Cultural Enlargement" of the EU and Europe's identity. Vol. 2: The Chain of Peripheries and the New Wider Europe.* Hauppauge, NY: Nova Science Publishers. Abridged paperback editions, 2006, are available under the following titles: *The West, Europe and the Muslim World* (Vol. 1), and *Towards a Wider Europe* (Vol. 2).

Inglehart, R. T. 1990. *Culture Shift in Advanced Industrial Societies.* Princeton, NJ: Princeton University Press.

———. 2007. "The Worldviews of Islamic Publics in Global Perspective." In *Values and perceptions of the Islamic and Middle Eastern Publics*, ed. M. Moaddel, 25–46). Houndmills, Basingstoke, Hampshire: Palgrave Macmillan.

Inglehart, R. T., and P. Norris. 2003. *Rising Tide: Gender Equality and Cultural Change Around the World.* Cambridge (UK), New York: Cambridge University Press.

Lewis J., K. Polanyi, and D. Kitchin, eds. 1972. *Christianity and the Social Revolution.* Freeport, NY: Books for Libraries Press.

Moaddel, M. 1994. Political Conflict in the World Economy: A Cross-National Analysis of Modernization and World-System Theories. *American Sociological Review* 59(2): 276–303.

———. 1996. The Social Bases and Discursive Context of the Rise of Islamic Fundamentalism: The Cases of Iran and Syria. *Sociological Inquiry* 66(3): 330.

———. 1998. Religion and Women: Islamic Modernism Versus Fundamentalism. *Journal for the Scientific Study of Religion* 37(1): 108.

———. 2002. The Study of Islamic Culture and Politics: An Overview and Assessment. *Annual Review of Sociology* 28: 359–386.

———. 2004. The Future of Islam after 9/11. *Futures* 36(9): 961–977.

———. 2005. *Islamic Modernism, Nationalism and Fundamentalism: Episode and Discourse.* Chicago: University of Chicago Press.

Müller, A., A. Tausch, and P. M. Zulehner, eds. 1999. *Global Capitalism, Liberation Theology and the Social Sciences: An Analysis of the Contradictions of Modernity at the Turn of the Millennium.* Huntington, NY: Nova Science Publishers. Paperback edition, 2000.

Noland, M. 2004. *Religion and Economic Performance.* Washington, DC: The Peterson Institute. Accessed at: http://www.petersoninstitute.org/publications/wp/03-8.pdf.

———. 2005 (June). *Explaining Middle Eastern authoritarianism* (Working Paper Series Number 05-5). Washington, DC: Institute for International Economics. Accessed at: http://www.iie.com/publications/wp/wp05-5.pdf.

Noland, M., and H. Pack. 2004 (June). *Islam, Globalization, and Economic Performance in the Middle East* (International Economics Policy Briefs Number PB04-4). Washington, DC: Institute for International Economics. Accessed at: http://www.iie.com/publications/pb/pb04-4.pdf.

PEW Research Center for the People & the Press. 2006 (June 22). *The Great Divide: How Westerners and Muslims View Each Other. Europe's Muslims More Moderate.* Washington, DC: PEW Global Attitudes Project. Accessed at: http://pewglobal.org/reports/display.php?ReportID=253.

Polanyi, K. 1957. *The Great Transformation: The Political and Economic Origins of Our Time*. Boston: Beacon.

———. 1979. *Öekonomie und Gesellschaft*. Frankfurt a.M.: Suhrkamp Taschenbuch Wissenschaft.

Savage, T. M. 2004. Europe and Islam: Crescent waxing, cultures clashing. *The Washington Quarterly*, 27(3): 25–50. Accessed at:http://www.twq.com/04summer/docs/04summer_savage.pdfsearch=%22crescent%20waxing%20savage%22.

Tausch, A. (with Fred Prager). 1993. *Towards a Socio-Liberal Theory of World Development*. Basingstoke and New York: Macmillan/St. Martin's Press.

———. 2003. "Social Cohesion, Sustainable Development and Turkey's Accession to the European Union: Implications from a Global Model." *Alternatives: Turkish Journal of International Relations* 2(1). Accessed at: http://www.alternativesjournal.net/ and http://www.alternativesjournal.net/volume2/number1/tausch.htm.

———. 2004. "Europe, the Muslim Mediterranean and the End of the Era of Global Confrontation." *Alternatives: Turkish Journal of International* Relations 3(4). Accessed at: http://www.alternativesjournal.net/volume3/number4/arno3.pdf.

———. 2005. "Is Islam Really a Development Blockade?" *Insight Turkey* 7(1): 124–135. Accessed at: http://papers.ssrn.com/sol3/papers.cfm?abstract_id=976588.

———. 2007. *Against Islamophobia: Quantitative Analyses of Global Terrorism, World Political Cycles and Center-Periphery Structures*. Hauppauge, NY: Nova Science Publishers.

———. 2007. Quantitative World System Studies Contradict Current Islamophobia: World Political Cycles, Global Terrorism, and World Development. *Alternatives: Turkish Journal of International* Relations 6(1, 2): 15–81. Accessed at: http://www.alternativesjournal.net/volume6/number1&2/tausch.pdf.

———. 2009. *What 1.3 Billion Muslims Really Think. An Answer to A Recent Gallup Study, Based on the "World Values Survey,"* Hauppauge, NY: Nova Science Publishers.

Tibi, B. 2007. The Totalitarianism of Jihadist Islamism and Its Challenge to Europe and to Islam. *Totalitarian Movements and Political* Religions 8(1): 35–54.

## NOTES

1. http://www.univie.ac.at/veil/Home3/index.php?id=22,0,0,1,0,0.

2. http://www.geocities.com/embracing_islam/ehrenfels.html.

3. http://www.huffingtonpost.com/amitai-etzioni/is-secularism-the-best-an_b_44911.html.

4. I would like to thank my dear friend Professor Tausch for this beautiful foreword. Iranian readers may not be very familiar with his work in the fields of sociology and liberation theology, but his main outlets for publication in the Muslim world—*Alternatives: Turkish Journal of International Relations* (freely accessible on the Internet) and *Insight Turkey* (published by the Ankara Center for Turkish Policy Studies [ANKAM])—are widely available.

# Introduction

Undoubtedly, any theory in the context of sociology is deeply intertwined with what Jeffery C. Alexander calls "Background Assumptions." Two significant assumptions that make up the delicate contours of theoretical deliberations are the milieus that constitute the domains of *weltanschauung* and *anthropology*. Allama Mohammad Taqi (Taghi) Jafari (also known as Allama Jafari) was one of the most distinguished social theorists of contemporary Iran who wrote extensively on various aspects of human sciences and philosophy as well as literature over five decades, from the early 1950s to the late 1990s. One of the most controversial questions since the Enlightenment has been the problem of reason and its (dis)connection to revelation or, to put it differently, the contrast between the humanist-centered worldview and the religious-centered *weltbild*. But within disciplinary contexts, we have gotten accustomed to reading Eurocentric takes on fundamental questions of humanities without venturing beyond the parameters of Eurocentrism. This lack of engagement on behalf of disciplinary scholars has turned into distorted professional ethics, which has paralyzed humanity on a global scale.

In other words, we as intellectuals do not know how to establish dialogue across cultural divides and engage with one another in a truly meaningful existential fashion, and this is applicable in a cruder manner to the general public around the globe. If this disengagement could be managed at the level of scholars, we would only have misunderstandings in a scholarly fashion, but now at the public level we are faced with sub-worlds where the "other" is viewed as a potential foe that should be terminated at any cost, and with whatever means. This is madness personified in the 21st century, and we are still unaware of its consequences.

To put it differently, the disengagements of Hegel with Mulla Ismael Xajuei or Durkheim with Mulla Mohammad Mehdi Naraghi and Habermas with Mehdi Haeri are lamentable, but the scope of the problem is manageable due to the nature of scholarly ethos. Now we are encountering a problem of a totally different character due to the dynamics of popular mentality, which is not equipped with abstract thinking. This, in and of itself, aggravates civilizational as well as cultural conflicts in a balkanized fashion. If Cartesian philosophers could afford ignoring Sadraian thinkers or vice versa, today such an approach would not work at all. In the absence of such engagement, we will not witness only disengagements. On the contrary, the option is conflict, and the scope of the clash is not confined to a clan but the whole globe could be a target, as Samuel P. Huntington demonstrated with his discussion about the fault lines in his theory of what he regarded as the impending clash of civilizations.

As Weber rightly discerned, the most controversial question that could cause vital differences, which may lead to bloody massacres, is the issue of value. In other words, the differences between various value systems have the potential to lead to serious disagreements with genocidal/biocidal/ecocidal consequences. This is another way of arguing that any theory of significance should clarify for us what the place of human beings is in the scheme of life since the query about values is a direct question about the dynamics of human self as an existential reality. Allama Jafari was a social theorist who was concerned about the destiny of the human person at four levels in an integral fashion—namely, Man as a social being, Man as a cosmic being, Man in a horizontal fashion, and Man in a vertical dimension. Of course the question of destiny has been dealt with by prominent disciplinary sociologists such as Gregor McLennan and Zygmund Bauman, but these outstanding secularist discourses are devoid of the quadruple dimensions that are discernible in the Jafarian frame of reference.

In the history of religions, we are able to detect five grand conceptions about religion in terms of the quiddity or "whatness" of religion as a phenomenon. These five approaches to religiosity are discernible in all world religions in various degrees, both contemporaneously and historically. The first one is religion defined in terms of jurisprudential credentials; the second is when religion is defined along gnostical ideals; the third is when religion is interpreted in light of philosophical deliberations; the fourth is when religion is defined in terms of science and scientific ideals; and the fifth is when religion is defined in terms of atheism, i.e., the conviction that the human person is unable of having belief beyond the temporal parameters of existence. All these approaches are discernible in the history of religions and even in the history of Iran and Islam. Allama Jafari seems to view the destiny of humanity in a religious fashion, but it is wrong to assume that his social theory is devoid of discursive reasoning or that his religiosity lacks complexity along the abovementioned lines. In other words, religion means "right choice" based on an "intelligible foundation," which is achievable through "pilgrimage"[1] and is disconnected from coercion, violence, and force. The "path of pilgrimage" can only be consolidated through "cordial intuition" and "existential efforts," and these require a high level of consciousness, which is not available to us due to the lack of a public educational system with such a broad and deep characteristic. The theory of "intelligible life" proposed by Allama Jafari seems to be an attempt in this direction and should not be treated as a jurisprudential interpretation of religion. Of course, the debates on religion and secularity are of great significance as we are approaching very interesting historical moments where from liberal corners the question of "post-secularism" is high on the agenda, and from Iran (as the bedrock of Religious Republicanism), we can now hear voices that are best defined as "post-Jurisprudentialism." There are issues that need to be noted lest we misunderstand each other about these sociological processes that will have global consequences in the epochs to come. Just as post-secularism does not mean the total destruction of everything that has been achieved during the hegemony of secularism, it is erroneous to believe that a post-jurisprudential era would willy-nilly entail the devastation of all things associated with religion or religiosity or, even worse, the emergence of a liberalistic interpretation of religion—which has failed historically due to the failure of Liberalism in the core countries of Europe. However, it would surely entail a reorientation (in terms of values) and reorganization (in terms of institutions), both in the East and the West, as depicted in *The Great Transformation* by Karl Polanyi.

To understand the nature of Jafarian social thought and the contribution Allama Jafari has made to the world sociological body of knowledge, we need to make a comparison between the primordial school of social theory as embodied by people like Jafari, Muttahari, Beheshti, Shariati, Iqbal, Naghib al-Attas, and Imam Musa Sadr, and disciplinary sociology and the European tradition of social theory as represented by Habermas, Giddens, Goffman, and especially Karl Polanyi, who seems to share many fundamental principles with Allama Jafari, such as "immortality of human soul," "Rubberband Man" and "Naturalized Self," "centrality of consciousness," and "substantivism." Here I am not about to compare the social theories of Polanyi and Jafari, as this would require a totally different approach, but it is worth mentioning that Polanyi's "substantivism" could be compared to Jafari's "intelligibilism," as both are novel attempts in unearthing the complexities of human existence beyond the parameters of disciplinary sociological theories. I have tried to look at Jafari's social theory in relation to a few contemporary discourses in the opening chapter, but a separate work must be devoted to a study comparing Polanyi and Jafari, who seem to argue for the dynamics of spirituality in the constitution of self and society. As mentioned earlier, the question of anthropology occupies a pivotal place within Jafarian frame of reference, and it would not be an exaggeration to argue that his social theory is an anthropological approach to the question of human existence in all conceivable dimensions, such as the Natural, Cosmic, Inner, Social, and Historical domains. Jafari's anthropology is composed of two interrelated dimensions of "is" and "ought to be" (Jafari 1386, 17). He, like other primordial social thinkers such as Polanyi, believes in the dynamics of spirituality in the constitution of human reality and the reality of humanity. In other words, one of the most significant issues that should be taken into consideration in the primordial definition of human self is its spiritual inclination, which plays a vital role in the constitution of human beings *qua* being (Jafari 1386, 150–151).

In sum, the disciplinary social theory seems to be on the wrong track when sociologists assume that human beings should be independent from others and when the autonomy of self is defined in contradistinction to the Ultimate Reality, which in religious parlance is termed as God (Jafari 1386, 185). Autonomy is not possible unless the human self realizes its essential dependence on the Holy and also consciously strives in actualizing this creative (both in the sense that it is created and it is imaginatively original) reliance in the spirit of liberty (Jafari 1386, 186).

## NOTE

1. This is an equivalent term that I have chosen for *suluk* in transcendent philosophy, which does not reduce the "poetry of being" into "behaviour" by instead insisting on the integral fashion of complex human reality.

# Chapter One

# Biography

It would be very useful and instructive if we could write a comprehensive biography of Allama Jafari, as his entire adult life seemed to be focused on what Erich Fromm aptly termed as "The Art of Being," or what Zygmund Bauman called "The Art of Living." But until such research is undertaken by students of humanities and social sciences, we shall settle for a brief glance at Jafari's life, which could assist non-Iranian readers picture the man behind his ideas. I must hasten to add that the lack of such a biography is even felt in the Persian language. Unfortunately, Iranian scholars have not paid sufficient attention to the importance of biographical research on the lives of prominent contemporary philosophers, social theorists, and writers, which could enable students of humanities to see the whole picture about men like Allama Jafari. In other words, the "culture of negligence" has become our second nature, and this is visible in all aspects of Iranian society. Its burden becomes heavier and more unbearable with every passing day. However, here we shall attempt to highlight a few aspects of Allama Jafari's life, which hopefully can provide a glimpse into what Socrates considered "The Examined Life" that is worth living, which is how Allama Jafari viewed the project of "intelligible life" that crossed the shores of "natural life."

Allama Mohammad Taqi Jafari was born in 1923 in the city of Tabriz, northwest of Iran. He learned how to read and write from his mother even before he started school, so he began his formal education in the fourth grade. Indeed, his academic progress was wonderful from the very start, but it was Ayatollah Shahidi who actually realized how talented he was years later. After elementary school, Allama Jafari began to study at the Talebieh seminary, and then moved to Tehran and Qom, where he studied under some of the outstanding religious scholars of his time. When he heard about his mother's illness, he returned to Tabriz, where he attended Ayatollah Shahidi's classes. Soon, his teacher insisted that he should shift to Najaf, and he joined the Najaf School of theology at a very young age. He spent 11 years in Najaf and learned from great scholars. His progress was so spectacular that he was conferred with the highest degree of jurisprudence when he was only 23 years old. Shortly thereafter, he began teaching at Najaf.

His life in Najaf was very hard, as Allama Jafari's wife, the late Jamila Farshbaf Entezar, recalled: "During the hot summers, we were forced to live in cellars several meters under the ground. There were even snakes there, but they ate our leftover food, and never harmed us". His wife never left Allama Jafari's side during all the years of hardship. Very few really know how instrumental her role was in the life of this prominent Iranian social philosopher. Allama expressed his appreciation for her in a speech he gave after her death, in the following words:

> This lady lived with me for over 40 years, tolerating every problem we had [...]. She never stopped me, she always let me go on with what I did, neglecting her own wishes. She ought to be greatly appreciated, especially for those difficult Najaf years. And for all the forty years! I can indeed do nothing but thank her for all she did for me and pray that her soul rest in peace.

Allama Jafari had a close and long friendship with Mohammad Reza Muzaffar, the great philosopher, and Ahmad Amin, the renowned mathematician of Baghdad University and author of the book *Evolution in Islam*. He had a good grasp of other fields of knowledge, such as physics, aesthetics, sociology, history, psychology, and several others, and he constantly tried to be up-to-date in Western and European literature and sciences. His first book, *The Relationship between Man and the Universe*, which he wrote when he was in his late twenties, shows how he kept himself abreast with contemporary intellectual currents in science and literature. The book, which deals with physics and philosophy, indicates how seriously he considered the relationship between modernity and religion by being critical towards modernism while not shying away from shaking the grounds of dogmatism in terms of interpretation of the religious canon. It is significant to note that his style of criticism was that of a young Islamic academician who had been trained by the best Islamic scholars of his time, in a dialogical mode and engaging with intellectual currents in a scholarly fashion. Of course, one should not forget the decisive role of the religious worldview in shaping the contours of his thought and social theory, which reflect the vital significant of unicity as the guiding principle of knowledge. On an integral approach to the pursuit of knowledge, he had the following to say:

The true intellectual should always stay in touch with the vast sea of facts in the flow of time, and follow the command of reason, submit to the demand of causality and know the factors which are of decisive importance in the constitution of life in all its complex aspects.

Allama Jafari strongly believed in dialogue and intellectual engagement. Those who knew him well and had witnessed his long years of study and research would admit that nothing was more important to him than pursuing knowledge and engaging in debates and in challenging discussions. He often shifted from one field of science to another in search of answers to his incessant questions, and he spent most of his time reading the works of seminal thinkers from different intellectual traditions and religions as well as scientific journals that contained new scientific materials and ideas, which provided him again with new questions. As he used to often say:

> Questions are signs of eagerness on behalf of the inquirer who seeks to gain knowledge about unknown realities. Questions actually mean that the questioner is saying that he has encountered a dark point on his path toward knowledge, and is eager to overcome it. Thus, passing over the bridges and round turns of doubt that are a necessary part of the phenomenon we call asking is quite natural. In fact, we can say that on the long road to knowledge, the more bridges and turns we pass and cross with certainty, the better. That means facing many questions. There are very few people who do not know the importance of questions. In fact, if we accept that questions sometimes come in the form of movements and endeavors instead of words or written texts, we agree that no one can account for his life without employing questions.

That is why Allama Jafari treated anyone who stepped into his world of asking and answering in a kind, fatherly manner. As Abraham Maslow so eloquently put it in his *Toward a Psychology of Being*:

> If one factor of his permanent legacy was his cooperation with men and women who presented questions—which arose out of his burning, innate interest in answering questions—another was his affection and consideration toward human beings, as each individual presented for him an opportunity towards individuation and becoming, illustrating the wonderful possibilities that humanity could actualize. (Maslow 1968, 17)

As an explorer of anthropological domains, Allama Jafari endeavored to discover both the logic and poetry of human existence as accurately as possible. In this regard, he departed from the modernist episteme, which distinguishes between the realms of epistemology and ontology. The question of "practical philosophy" was not only an intellectual problem for him but also a "practical concern" in a vital fashion, which without alienation would rule supreme, as it does today. This is to say that Allama Jafari applied moral values in his ethical praxis by realizing them within his own ethos, as these values were indeed of value for anyone concerned with the possibility of self-realization within the context of human life.

Perhaps it was his moral excellence that helped him accomplish so much in a rather short period of time—Jafari wrote many books on a vast variety of fields, the most prominent of which are his 15-volume *Interpretation and Criticism of Rumi's Mathnavi*, and his 27-volume *Translation and Interpretation of the Nahj-ol-Balagheh*. These two major works contain his most important thoughts and ideas in fields such as anthropology, sociology, ethics, philosophy, and mysticism.

Another point worth mentioning about Allama Jafari's life is the seriousness on which he always insisted. "With the meager allowance we got from the seminary in Najaf," he recalled, "sometimes I had to choose whether to spend my money on food or books. I always bought books instead." Having grown up and spent his years as a student in poverty, he continued to avoid luxury and wealth even when his academic state allowed him some economic comfort. His character could not adapt to affairs other than scientific or academic; his main goal was to find a way to remedy the crisis of identity and answer the questions to which students at universities and theological schools were seeking solutions. This was the most important thing on Allama Jafari's mind.

Allama Jafari never withered from his ideals; neither fashion nor ideological trend could distract him from the goal he had set for himself from the very early days when he entered Najaf—of how to realize "intelligible life" both individually and collectively beyond the traditional borders of religions and cultures or received traditions of the East and the West. Despite all the philosophical issues on his mind, he always insisted on upholding ideals such as duty, responsibility, and commitment. As a Jewish woman recalled:

> Some years ago, we had a legal problem, and there was nothing we could do about it. We needed help, but since we were Jewish it was hard to find someone to trust. Then we thought of asking Allama Jafari to help us. We went to his house. He welcomed us warmly. He put a lot of time into carefully studying our case. He felt we might be treated unjustly, so he wrote a letter to the judicial officials, which helped a great deal in solving our problem.

Another of Allama Jafari's characteristics was his belief that fields like knowledge and thought are truly endless—which is the only thing that can account for his amazingly vast set of works—on subjects as diverse as aesthetics, philosophical analysis, knowledge, sociology, artistic analysis, cognition, and mental reception.

Indeed, Allama Mohammad Taqi Jafari was one of the rare thinkers of recent centuries who attempted to marry reason and revelation or contingency and permanence. This was because he truly believed in renewing one's thoughts, which, in turn, reflected how he understood the question of unity and diversity or universalism and particularism. The question of human rights was of importance to him, not because of political considerations but as a matter of principle, which he conceptualized as the principle of "common human culture," or as he put it: "Beyond their appearance, all human cultures have a lot in common and are inseparably associated. We need to understand the logic of diversity versus unity by realizing the poetry of unicity in the constitution of self and society."

Such ideas arose out of the events and developments that occurred through the course of time. There is no doubt that Allama Jafari was a steadfast advocate of taking seriously the challenges of the time and the transformations brought about by time. In Iran, this question came to be conceptualized by various thinkers such as Allama Tabatabai, Muttahari, Beheshti, Taleghani, Chamran, Bazargan, Jafari, Shariati, and so on, as one that concerned religion and the exigencies of the time.

To correctly understand Allama Jafari's position, we should compare him with his contemporaries in the 20th century, such as Karl Polanyi, Bertrand Russell, Erich Fromm, Abraham Maslow, Karl Jaspers, Abdul-Salam, Alfred North Whitehead, Ahmad Amin, and many others, who directly or indirectly engaged with him. His viewpoints were sought by leading researchers all around the world. It was most likely his free-mindedness that gave him such an important stature. It should not be surprising, therefore, when Greek thinkers remember him as a man who "never rejected anyone" and as "a teacher, not a judge."

In sum, the name of Allama Mohammad Taqi Jafari is well known in the fields of logic, metaphysics, philosophy, literature, jurisprudence, mysticism, history, and the philosophy of science in Iran and, to some extent, in the world of Islam. His work in the fields of aesthetics, ethics, education, and the philosophy of religion has attracted the interest of many serious students. However, very little attention has been paid to his discussion of social theory. Yet, as a matter of fact, he had been interested in social problems throughout his life. Jafari's theory of "intelligible life" stresses the social factor. It is worth noting that he delivered long lectures on sociology and sociological problems, which were collected by his students, such as Mr. Bonakdariyan in the 1970s, and later on submitted to me by Allama Jafari's son, Alireza Jafari, at the Center for Jafari Studies in Tehran. These exclusive works on sociology should be studied and compared with disciplinary sociological currents as they could probably shed valuable light on the state of sociological imagination in Iran. Of course this is a concern that we cannot deal with in this study, but in the near future, we hope to work on this aspect of Allama Jafari's thought, too.[1]


# NOTE

1. I thank Allama Jafari's son, Mr. Alireza Jafari, from the Center for Jafari Studies in Tehran, who provided me with this biographical material.

*Chapter Two*

# Relocating the
# Jafarian Perspective

## INTRODUCTION

It would not be an exaggeration to consider Allama Jafari as the father of studies on "Conscience," based on primordial considerations within contemporary social theory. Almost all of his ideas are meant to explain the mechanisms and poetry of conscience as a human science problem. In order to be able to understand the importance of Allama Jafari's considerations on the question of conscience, one needs to re-read recent reappraisals of some epistemological aspects of modern/secular metaphysics of being and ontology. In other words, it would be instructive to examine a few trends within the social theory of self and being, which have come with novel ideas about the significance of conscience in relation to science. If we view the matter from this perspective, the importance of Allama Jafari's engagement with the question of conscience could have significant consequences for sociology and social theory, and even for our theories with regard to the philosophy of science and the cosmology of being.

As Sean Kelly rightly notes:

The last few decades have seen the emergence of a growing body of literature devoted to a critique of the so-called "old" or "Cartesian-Newtonian" paradigm which, in the wake of the prodigious successes of modern natural science, came to dominate the full range of authoritative intellectual discourses and their associated worldviews. Often coupled with a materialistic, and indeed atomistic, metaphysics, this paradigm has been guided by the methodological principle of reductionism. The critics of reductionism have tended to promote various forms of holism, a term which, perhaps more than any other, has served as the rallying cry for those who see themselves as creators of a "new paradigm." More

7

recently, the notion of complexity has been taken up by the more scientifically informed representatives of the new paradigm, without, however, sufficient awareness of the fact that what excites the scientists is the possibility of . . . reducing the phenomenon of complexity to fundamentally simple, essentially atomistic, operational counters.

The situation is quite otherwise, however, in the work of renowned French thinker Edgar Morin, whose professional life has been devoted to elucidating the irreducible character of genuine complexity. Because his work has yet to reach a wide global audience, most new paradigm thinkers . . . have not had the benefit of his masterful critique of reductionism, or simplification, as he prefers to call it. Nevertheless, the principles of complex thinking which inform this critique are . . . essential for any coherent theoretical challenge to the still dominant paradigm of simplification.

At the forefront of such a challenge, and in many ways the herald of the new paradigm, is the relatively new movement of transpersonal social theory within the frame of disciplinary psychology. Responding to the revolution in consciousness associated with the 1960s counterculture—which involved widespread interest in "altered" states of consciousness, oriental philosophies and spiritual disciplines, [perennial orientations within philosophy and mysticism], ecological awareness, social activism, and speculative or "fringe" science—Abraham Maslow, Stanislav Grof, Anthony Sutich, and James Fadiman proposed the term "transpersonal" to describe a new, "fourth force" psychology (the first three forces being behaviorism, psychoanalysis, and humanistic psychology) [within the wider context of social theory and philosophy]. The prefix trans points to the concept of transcendence implied in a whole class of experiences involving "an extension of identity beyond both individuality and personality" (Walsh and Vaughan 1980, 16).

In taking seriously such experiences, transpersonal theory has been compelled to transcend the disciplinary boundaries of mainstream social theory. On the one hand, it has opened itself to the reality of "Spirit" in its many forms (as revealed in myths and visions, meditation and other contemplative disciplines, in philosophy, art, doctrines and rituals), and so has drawn freely from such disciplines as religious studies, cultural anthropology, and comparative philosophy. On the other hand, in its attempt to articulate more comprehensive and coherent models of the psyche that are capable of accommodating experiences of transcendence, transpersonal social theory has also led the way in exploring the fruitfulness of conceptual analogues drawn from the leading edge of the natural sciences (the new physics, evolutionary biology, Systems Theory). In what follows, I will explore the transdisciplinary excursions of transpersonal social theory, with an eye on the extent to which its theoretical innovations embody the principles of complex thinking—i.e. the dialogic, the holographic principle, and recursivity. It is my belief that, while transpersonal [psychological inclinations within social theory have] already attained a level of considerable theoretical maturity, it would be greatly assisted in fulfilling its transdisciplinary promise were it to enter into dialogue with the paradigm of complexity as articulated by Morin.

Although the official beginnings of the transpersonal movement date only from 1969, significant theoretical advances were already underway at the turn of the 20th century [in the West and, earlier, in other civilizational contexts]. In 1903, just three years after the publication of Freud's *Interpretation of Dreams*, Frederic Myers, in his massive . . . *Human Personality and Its Survival of Bodily Death*, proposed a radically transpersonal view of the human psyche based on an enormous quantity of data collected by the British Society for Psychical Research. Whether or not one agrees with Myers's conclusions regarding the probability of some kind of personal immortality, his subtle musings on the complex character of the "subliminal self" deserve far greater attention than they have hitherto received [within social psychology, social theory and philosophy]. Steering a middle course between, on the one hand, the "old-fashioned" or "common sense" view of the psyche as organized around the "unity of the Ego" and, on the other hand, the then current experimental view of the psyche as a biologically driven "co-ordination" of disparate elements, Myers concluded: "I regard each man as at once profoundly unitary and almost infinitely composite, as inheriting from earthly ancestors a multiplex and "colonial" organism—polyzoic and perhaps polyspychic [sic] in an extreme degree; but also as ruling and unifying that organism by a soul or spirit absolutely beyond our present analysis—a soul which has originated in a spiritual environment . . . which even while embodied subsists in that environment; and which will subsist therein after the body's decay."

Writing in his 1901 Gifford Lectures, *The Varieties of Religious Experience*, William James regarded Myers's concept of the subliminal or "transmarginal" Self as "the most important step forward that has occurred in psychology [social theory] since I have been a student of that science . . ." (James 1901–02/1977, 234). Commenting on the implications of the transmarginal self, James writes: "It is that our normal waking consciousness, rational consciousness as we call it, is but one special type of consciousness, whilst all about it, parted from it by the filmiest of screens, there lie potential forms of consciousness entirely different. . . . No account of the universe in its totality can be final which leaves these other forms of consciousness quite disregarded . . . . [they] may determine attitudes though they cannot furnish formulas, and open a region though they fail to give a map. . . ."

Looking back on his own experiences and investigations of this region, James feels that, "they all converge towards a kind of insight to which I cannot help ascribing some metaphysical significance. It is as if the opposites of the world, whose contradictoriness and conflict make our difficulties and troubles, were melted into unity. Not only do they, as contrasted species, belong to one and the same genus, but one of the species, the nobler and better one, is itself the genus and so soaks up and absorbs its opposite into itself. This is a dark saying, I know, when thus expressed in terms of common logic. . . . those who have ears to hear, let them hear" (ibid., 374).

It is telling that, in recognizing ordinary consciousness as embedded within what he elsewhere describes as multiple "fields" of indeterminate extent, James is driven to transcend "the terms of common logic" and invoke an epistemology that can encompass the unity, or co-presence, of opposites. When knowledge of organization (in this case, the organization of consciousness or the psyche) reaches the threshold of complexity, as Morin so often demonstrates, one cannot avoid a corresponding reformation in the organization of knowledge. Such a reformation, as we shall see, is a characteristic trait of the transpersonal project.

C. G. Jung . . . clearly had ears to hear, and struggled for over half a century to lay the groundwork for a truly complex psychology [social theory] of self (and various layers of being). His first move in this direction involved trying to account for the fact that the perspectives of Freud and Adler, though mutually antagonistic, were equally complementary. They were, as Morin would say, dialogically related (see Morin 1977, 80). While one or the other perspective might prove more therapeutically advantageous, depending upon the specific needs of the individual client, a truly coherent and comprehensive model of the psyche must be able to accommodate both. Jung concluded that Freud's perspective, which emphasizes the sexual instinct, is primarily object-oriented—or extraverted, as he proposed to call it—while Adler's, which emphasizes the power drive, is introverted. This fundamental typological distinction allowed Jung to make sense not only of the conflict between Freud and Adler, but also of the analogous tension running throughout the history of ideas (with the perennial dispute between materialists and idealists or secularists and religionists, for instance).

A second tension with which Jung struggled, and which clearly signaled his break with Freud, concerns the dialogical relation between the reductive-analytic and the prospective-synthetic perspectives on the meaning of psychological symptoms that are of significance for the constitution of self. Again, Jung always granted that certain cases are best approached from a classical analytic perspective, with its reduction to . . . the oedipal conflict. In other cases, however, such a reduction does violence to the future-oriented drive for meaning and wholeness—a drive which Jung considered as equally fundamental as the sex drive or the drive for power. . . .

The goal toward which, however implicitly, the psyche's symbolic productions seemed to point was the actualization of a potential wholeness the phenomenology of which, though always in some way specific to the individual in question, nevertheless suggested an invariant deep structure. Jung proposed the term "individuation" to describe the psyche's process of self-actualization and the term "Self" for that which is actualized. The wholeness of the Self is clearly complex in character, which is why, says Jung, that "it can only be described in antinomial terms" (Jung 1953–79). It is "both ego and non-ego, subjective and objective, individual and collective. It is the "uniting symbol" which epitomizes the total union of opposites" (Jung 1953–79, 16:474). Though Jung used several phrases to describe the nature of the Self—from the "psyche in its totality" and the "more compendious personality" to "the god within" (in this sense making the association with the theological notion of the *imago dei*, the Atman, and the Tao)—the most succinct formula . . . is that of the Self as *complexio oppositorum* (see Jung 1953–79, 6:790; 9ii:355, 423; 11:283, 716; 12:259).

Jung recognized that the concept of the Self is a "transcendental postulate" which, "although justified empirically does not allow of scientific proof" (Jung 1953–79, 7:404). This "step beyond science"—by which we can understand the conception of science advocated by the paradigm of reductionism or simplification—"is an unconditional requirement of the psychological development I sought to depict, because without this postulate I could give no adequate formulation of the psychic processes that occur empirically" (ibid.). (Kelly 2009)

This is a point that has been raised by Allama Jafari, too, and will be touched upon later on.

Corresponding to the concept of the Self as "transcendental postulate" is Jung's notion of the "transcendent function" which, in general terms, is the cognitive process that "arises from the union of conscious and unconscious contents" (Jung 1953–79, 8:131). This function represents a creative response on the part of the individuating ego when it finds itself trapped between two seemingly irreconcilable positions—for instance, between the promptings of intuition or feeling and the voice of reason, or between the security of habitual values and the lure of innovative change. In such a conflict situation, the confrontation of the two positions "generates a tension charged with energy and creates a living, third thing—not a logical stillbirth in accordance with the principle *tertium non datur* but a movement out of the suspension between opposites, a living birth that leads to a new level of being, a new situation" (ibid., 189). There now emerges "a new content, constellated by thesis and antithesis in equal measure and standing in a compensatory relation to both" (Jung 1953–79, 6:825). This comes very close to what Morin sees as perhaps the greatest virtue of complex thinking—namely, "the aptitude of enveloping the anti in the meta" (Morin 1982, 317). What this means is "not letting oneself be dissociated by contradiction and antagonism . . . but on the contrary, integrating it in a whole (ensemble) where it may continue to ferment, where, without losing is [sic] destructive potential, it acquires at the same time a constructive possibility" (ibid., 318). (Kelly 2009)

This integral approach to the question of self bears great resemblance to Allama Jafari's view on the "Conscience" as the *Fontes Vitae* of humanity in its authentically emancipative fashion (Jafari 1381, 305) or his idea about "higher conscience" that is reflected by the great prophets, mystics, and thinkers such as Tolstoy, Shakespeare, Victor Hugo, Dostoeveky, Rumi, and Socrates. (Jafari 1381, 304). In this regard, it would be exciting to explore how, for instance, Stanislav Grof's (1985) view on the "holotropic" approach to self-exploration is, or could be, connected to Allama Jafari's view on Vijdan as the true source of self-discovery. Allama Jafari thinks that Vijdan drives one toward a directed/purposeful divine target, and Grof's understanding of the holotropic approach is based on a pristine reading of holotropy (from the Greek *holos* or "whole" and *trepein* or "moving in the direction of something"). These resemblances have not been researched yet and need to be explored inter-civilizationally in order to explicate the deep-seated issues that could affect the very textures of self, society, and global coexistence in our troubled times.

Within the general context of social theory,

The complexification of psychology evident in the early transpersonal models of the psyche proposed by Myers, James, and Jung, received unexpected clinical-experiential confirmation in the 1950s and 60s through the pioneering psychedelic research of Stanislav Grof, one of the [creative] founders of the transpersonal movement. The experiential data on the effects of LSD gathered by Grof and his colleagues in Prague, and subsequently confirmed through thousands of drug-free sessions of holotropic breathwork, totally undermined the classic assumptions of Grof's materialistic, atheistic, and classical Freudian training. Deep, experiential engagement with the psyche, though it confirmed the relative truth of Freud's "biographical-recollective" view of the unconscious, also revealed deeper and subtler realms, including the Rankian . . . unconscious, the Jungian-archetypal, and beyond. Human beings, Grof writes, show a peculiar ambiguity which somewhat resembles the particle-wave dichotomy of light and subatomic matter. In some situations, they can be successfully described as separate material objects and biological machines, whereas in others they manifest the properties of vast fields of consciousness that transcend the limitations of space, time, and causality. There seems to be a fundamental dynamic tension between these two aspects of human nature, which reflects the ambiguity between the part and the whole that exists all through the cosmos on different levels of reality (Grof 1985, 344).

Grof was the first [social theorist within the transpersonal psychological context] to suggest that the holographic model which David Bohm had proposed for the new physics and Karl Pribram for brain research was equally fruitful for the realm of the psyche. According to Morin, the holographic principle—which involves the recognition that "the parts are in the whole which is in the parts" (see Morin 1986, 104)—is an essential ingredient of complex thinking. While ordinary, or "hylotropic," consciousness "involves the experience of oneself as a solid physical entity with definite boundaries and a limited sensory range, living in three-dimensional space and linear time" (Grof 1985, 345), "holotropic" consciousness "involves identification with a field of consciousness with no definite boundaries which has unlimited experiential access to different aspects of reality without the mediation of the senses" (ibid., 346).

Experiences in the holotropic mode systematically support a set of assumptions diametrically different from that characteristizing the hylotropic mode: the solidity and discontinuity of matter is an illusion generated by a particular orchestration of events in consciousness; time and space are ultimately arbitrary; the same space can be simultaneously occupied by many objects; the past and the future can be brought experientially into the present moment; one can experience oneself in several places at the same time; one can experience several temporal frameworks simultaneously; being a part is not incompatible with being the whole; something can be true and untrue at the same time; form and emptiness are interchangeable; and others (ibid.)

Clearly, holotropic experiences constitute a serious challenge to the paradigm of simplification. They demand an honoring not only of the holographic principle, but also of the dialogic as well insofar as holotropic experiences tend to exist in a state of "fundamental dynamic tension" with respect to ordinary, hylotropic consciousness. While Grof considers neurotic and psychotic phenomena to be the result of "an unresolved conflict between the two modes" (ibid., 400), he envisions the possibility of a "higher sanity" for individuals "who have achieved a balanced interplay of both complementary . . . modes of consciousness" (ibid., 401).

While Grof, like Jung before him, sought to expand and [make more complex] his model of the psyche to accommodate the empirical data with which, as a clinician and researcher, he was faced, Ken Wilber, the most ambitious and formidable theoretician of the transpersonal movement, is the first to explicitly and intentionally to overstep the disciplinary boundaries of scientific [human sciences]. In his first book, *The Spectrum of Consciousness* (1977), Wilber argued for the partiality and one-sidedness of the major schools of [social theory in general, and psychology in particular], each of which was seen to correspond to a distinct "band" of the consciousness spectrum. The higher wavelengths of the spectrum, moreover, transcend psychology altogether, and it is to the world's philosophical and spiritual traditions that we must turn for indications of their nature (as Myers, James, Jung, and Grof, in their own way, also suggested). (Kelly 2009)

The same was proposed vehemently by Allama Jafari in his discussions on "Conscience" and its role in the emergence of universal humanity and peaceful societies.

In his 1983 book, *Eye to Eye*, Wilber called for a "transcendental paradigm" or "overall knowledge quest that would include not only the 'hard ware' of physical sciences but also the 'soft ware' of philosophy and [social theory]/psychology and the 'transcendental ware' of mystical-spiritual religion" (Wilber 1983, 1). Alongside the spectrum model, and eventually more or less replacing it in importance, Wilber appealed to the "perennial" philosophical notion of the "Great Chain of Being," whose major "links" are Matter, Life, Mind, and Spirit, or physiosphere, biosphere, noosphere, and theosphere. Coupled with the metaphor of the Great Chain is the master-concept of holarchy, which Wilber adopted, and creatively adapted, from Systems Theory and certain strands of evolutionary biology. This concept, which itself implies the idea of a nested hierarchy of spheres within spheres, is somewhat at odds with the Great Chain metaphor, which rather suggests the idea of sequentially and externally related "links." Wilber admits that "we can use metaphors of 'levels' or 'ladders' or 'strata' . . . only if we exercise a little imagination in understanding the complexity that is actually involved" (Wilber 1995, 19). At his best, Wilber succeeds admirably in doing just that. In his discussion of the Nondual character of the Absolute, for instance, Wilber recognizes that "Reality is not just Summit (*omega*) and not just Source (*alpha*), but is Suchness—the timeless and ever-present Ground which is equally and fully present in and as every single being, high or low, ascending or descending, effluxing or refluxing" (ibid., 347).

Despite, however, Wilber's occasional stressing of the equipotency in the cosmic economy of hierarchy and heterarchy (or depth and span) and Ascent and Descent (or purpose and play), he still insists that the noosphere contains the biosphere, but not the reverse (and that the theosphere contains them both, but not the reverse). In this, and certain other respects, although still highly pertinent to the transdisciplinary [as well as intercivilizational] project, Wilber's paradigm is insufficiently spiced, as it were, with the essential ingredients of complex thinking. His understanding of holarchical integration (the higher includes the lower) gives expression to only half of the holographic principle (which implies that the lower also includes the higher). By the same token, Wilber does not seem to recognize that the various links in the Great Chain are not only holarchically, but also dialogically, related. As I have similarly argued (see Kelly 1993) with respect to Hegel, holarchical integration, as Wilber advocates it, is colored by an introverted, idealist bias towards the auto (or ego)-logic of Spirit over the eco-logic of nature. This bias obscures the degree to which the "higher" (mind or Spirit) sometimes not only does not include, but actively represses the "lower" (the body, Nature; see Kelly 1998). In such cases, the whole, as Morin would say, is not all (see Morin 1977, 123ff.). Also obscured is the paradoxical manner in which mind and spirit are subtly embedded within, and often manifest powerfully through, the body and nature. . . . And this, again, despite the fact that Wilber can claim . . . "If spirit is completely transcendent, it is also completely immanent. I am firmly convinced that if a new and comprehensive paradigm is ever to emerge, that paradox will be its heart" (Wilber 1983, 293).

The ability of the mind to countenance this paradox (and its corollaries) demands the mobilization of what Wilber calls "vision-logic" which, he writes, "is a higher holon that operates upon (and thus transcends) its junior holons, such as simple rationality itself." As such, vision-logic can hold in mind contradictions, it can unify opposites, it is dialectical and non-linear, and it weaves together what otherwise appear to be incompatible notions, as long as they relate together in the new and higher holon, negated in their partiality but preserved in their positive contributions (Wilber 1995, 185).

This description leaves no doubt that vision-logic, as Wilber conceives of it, is more or less identical with the Hegelian dialectic and its process of "sublation" (*aufheben*). While Morin honors Hegel for having recognized, with the dialectic, "the existence of a principle of negativity which transforms all things, all beings, all acts into their opposites" (Morin 1980, 82), he faults Hegel for considering contradiction a transitory "moment" of the *Aufhebung*, a moment which is ultimately annulled in the "synthesis" of the third term (see Morin 1982, 289). Wilber's vision-logic is subject to the same strictures, particularly insofar as it subserves the idealist metaphysics associated with the root metaphor of the Great Chain of Being. Although the notion of vision-logic represents a significant step beyond the formal-operational thinking typical of the mature . . . mental ego, it must, like the Hegelian dialectic, "itself be sublated in a dialogic . . . that instigates the interaction, through the joining in a manner at once complementary . . . and antagonistic, of two logics—auto-logic and eco-logic" (Morin 1980, 82).

In his most recent writings, Wilber has combined the Great Chain metaphor with, and embedded it within, a "Kosmic mandala" consisting of two intersecting axes—Interior/Exterior and Individual/Collective—which, when combined, yield four quadrants or world spaces: the intentional (interior/individual), the cultural (interior/collective), the behavioral (exterior/individual), and the social (exterior/collective). Though it is possible, and indeed [basically crucial occasionally], to consider discrete "holons" as they manifest in one or the other quadrant, Wilber insists that any truly "integral," or we might say "complex," methodology must proceed on the basis of an "all-quadrant, all-level" approach. "This is a methodology," he writes, of "phenomenologically and contemporaneously tracking the various levels and lines in each of the quadrants and then correlating their overall relations, each to all of the others, and in no way trying to reduce any to the others" (Wilber 1997, 91). While I cannot agree more strongly, it is once again unclear just how such a methodology squares with his strict adherence to the perennialist version of holarchical integration where Mind (the Interior, or "left" hand quadrants) includes Matter (the Exterior, or "right" hand quadrants), but not the reverse.

Toward the end of the first volume of his monumental Kosmos trilogy, Wilber poses the following questions: "Can we not see Spirit as the Life of Evolution and the Love of Kosmos itself . . . ? Does not the refluxing movement of God and the effluxing movement of the Goddess embrace the entire Circle of Ascent and Descent? Can we not . . . see that Spirit always manifests in all four quadrants equally? Is not Spirit here and now in all its radiant glory, eternally present as every I and every We and every It?" (Wilber 1995, 522).

It is in passages such as these that Wilber comes closest to realizing a truly integral or complex point of view. Though lacking a sufficiently dialogical grasp of the relations involved, his claim that "the circle of Ascending and Descending energies must always be unbroken" (Wilber 1995, 326) does suggest a recognition of the principle of recursivity which, along with the dialogic and the holographic principle, is one of Morin's essential ingredients of complex thinking. According to Morin, a process is recursive when it "causes/produces the effects/products necessary for its own regeneration" (Morin 1981, 162). It is "the circuitous process whereby the ultimate effect or product becomes the initial element or first cause" (Morin 1977, 186). The recursivity evident on the metaphysical plane with the relation AscentàDescent (and DescentàAscent) is mirrored on the psychological plane in the relation personalàtranspersonal (and transpersonalàpersonal), as well on the methodological or disciplinary plane with the relation scienceàspirituality (and spiritualityàscience). In contrast to the situation where Ascent, the transpersonal, and spirituality would sublate their respective correlates in a "higher" (idealist) synthesis, a truly complex (meta) point of view would insure that the "Great Circle," as Wilber calls it, remain unbroken. For this to happen, however, the concepts of holism (or holarchy) and the Nondual, though cardinal insights in their own right, will have to be tempered with the dialogic, the holographic principle, and the principle of recursivity.

We have seen that what drives transpersonal [social theory] in the direction of complexity is its focus on transcendence (of the mental ego and of psychology's disciplinary closure). Let me conclude with a few words on how the concept of spiritual transcendence appears to function in Morin's articulation of the emerging paradigm of complexity. On a first reading, it might seem that Morin makes no room for transcendence, at least not in the sense of Wilber's holarchical ontology. Morin recognizes no theosphere, or Absolute Spirit, which includes as it transcends the phenomenal world studied by the various sciences (whether natural or human). He is unambiguous in his rejection of the religions of salvation, whether otherworldly or this worldly. "There is no salvation," Morin writes, "in the sense of religions that promise personal immortality. There is no earthly salvation, as promised by the communist religion—that is, a social solution—in which the lives of all and everyone would be freed from misfortune, uncertainty, and tragedy. We must forsake this salvation radically and definitively" (Morin 1998, 134).

And yet Morin does recognize that, though the human condition is irrevocably "this-worldly and bound to the fate of the Earth," it nonetheless "also involves a quest for the beyond. Not a beyond outside of the world, but a beyond relative to the *hic et nunc*, to misery and misfortune, an unknown beyond that is proper to the unknown adventure" (ibid., 135). It is in this sense of transcendence as an imminent "beyond" that Morin is able to envision the possibility, and even the necessity, of a third type of religion—not a religion of salvation, but a religion of fellowship, freedom, and love. In such a religion, "the absence of God would reveal an omnipresent mystery." Such a religion "would be without revelation . . . a religion of love . . . of compassion . . . , although without the salvation of the immortal/risen self or deliverance through the dissipation of self" (ibid., 142). Just how we experience, and make sense of, the "omnipresent mystery" of the immanent beyond is, of course, a central concern of transpersonal social theory with traditional psychological concerns. Although, as we have seen, its various formulations of human selfhood—whether Myers's and James's subliminal or transmarginal Self, Jung's Self as *complexio oppositorium*, Grof's holotropic, or Wilber's holarchical Self—all represent significant attempts in coming to terms with the complex character of the immanent beyond, much remains to be explored. Transpersonal [social theory] is barley [sic] three decades old, and it will doubtless continue to mature in the direction of greater theoretical subtlety and sophistication. (Kelly 2009)

If it is to carry on, and fulfill an intercivilizationally beneficial role in the contemporary globalizing catastrophe-inclined milieu, one needs to enrich one's perspective through comparatively inter/transdisciplinary as well as non-disciplinary avenues, as we are living in a time where parallel times and spaces are at work in shaping our realities, imaginations, and so on. The changes brought about by transpersonal social theorists in regard to our understanding of self and transcendence, when coupled with the philosophy of conscience explored by Allama Jafari in the context of the metaphysics of science, may be able to bring about a Copernican revolution in relation to our understanding about the sources of "Inner Freedom," "Personality," "Human Conscience," and "Man as an expression of the Infinite" (Jafari 1381, 307).

Last but not least, it should be emphasized that prior to modernity we could think of world in terms of distinct civilizations, traditions, religions, denominations, nations, societies, states, continents and cultures, but today, although we can still think of the respective distinctiveness of each and every one of these entities, nevertheless it would be futile to seek to fathom them in isolation as we are in the midst of an intercivilizational project where all the agents and players are in constant conscious or unconscious interaction. So, it would be intellectually more beneficial and coexistentially more benevolent to transform the scope of our unawareness into active consciousness as self-consciousness, like God-consciousness, is of great significance for the emergence of the good life.

In other words, it is high time to change the status quo in our education in our universities by turning to global educational consciousness through exposing the mind to all relevant traditions that have contributed and are still contributing to the constant emergence of intercivilizational global reality. This cannot be brought about unless we get engaged with those intellectuals who have been interacting with the global emerging reality—not through Western rationality but via their own distinct intellectual traditions. The primordial intellectual tradition is one prime example in this regard which has been part of the contemporary sociological tradition as well as a great contributor to the emergence of intercivilizational dialogue in the context of the humanities and social sciences. Now the question is: Where does Allama Jafari stand in the broad context of *les sciences humaines*?

There is no doubt that the disciplinary form of human sciences emerged in the West, most particularly in France, Germany, and England and later on in America. I emphasize the term "particularly," as, for instance, the discipline of sociology in Turkey or political science in Iran emerged a century before then in Canada, New Zealand, or Australia, which are sometimes collectively put in the same category as "Western," which gives a totally unrealistic picture of the growth of social sciences globally. However, what is doubtful, though still widespread among social scientists and historiographers who portray images of the histories of each discipline within the pantheon of human sciences, is the notion of "relevant debates" that mainly starts from secular Western thinkers and ends with them, too.

In other words, when you pick up any theoretical or historiographical work on social sciences, it is very difficult to distinguish between "Western" and "global," as though these two terms should mean one and the same thing, even though the theorists claim that they are arguing about something extra-Western and all-inclusive. But this is difficult to substantiate as long as we do not hear about other voices and disallow the emergence of other relevant issues within the pantheon of *Kulturwissenschaften.* I have argued on this question elsewhere in more detail and here would like to settle for this concise detour and conclude with a point that would assist me in presenting Allama Jafari as a highly relevant social theorist and contemporary philosopher who engaged in various aspects of humanities in general, and human sciences in particular. To substantiate this claim, we now turn to his works and see what he has to say about "human sciences" or, as he puts it in Persian, *Ulum Ensani.*

For years, Allama Jafari stated that he had been

> researching various aspects of human sciences, and many times came across the word "conscience" and pondered upon it for hours, but, sadly, I have to tell you that I could not find anything essentially convincing about the disciplinary approaches provided by the researchers on this question as I found most of them have been extremely concerned with highly expert-oriented subtleties . . . without an enlightening end in sight. But, as I thought more of this question and introspectively analyzed my own inner data, I found out that this is a highly relevant question and, as a matter of fact, could prove to be one of the most significant issues of human existence, if understood rightly. With this new insight, I restarted my research on this question by looking at the works of contemporary philosophers, psychologists and psychoanalysts as far as I could . . . but my search did not lead me to an enlightening state as I found out that most of these discourses are devoid of vital aspects as they are mainly conceptual devices to explain conceptual problems constructed by earlier thinkers without any existential understanding. . . . Now, I don't want to argue that they all have been mistaken, but I would like to emphasize that their discourses did not convince me about what I have already found as highly significant and vitally important for the existence of the human being in contrast to animals—which eat, sleep, cry, laugh, mate, reproduce and die. In other words, if we agree that Man is his own owner/possessor and is able to think and be free, then what the contemporary secular thinkers have argued is not sufficient. (Jafari 2002, 13–14)

This rather lengthy quote perfectly demonstrates that Allama Jafari was conscious about modern/secular discourses as well as other contemporary discourses, such as those by Russian thinkers; Indian wisdom philosophers; Western poets; writers such as Shakespeare, Victor Hugo, and Dante; and ancient Greek and Chinese thinkers, such as Socrates and Confucius. Apart from this, one can discern his serious concern about human sciences as they are understood within the disciplinary framework of contemporary academia. Now, what he thinks of human sciences as a modern disciplinary episteme is beyond the primary concern of this author in this introductory chapter, but this was intended to display an undeniable fact about non-disciplinary approaches to disciplinary problems within human sciences by many non-secular or/and Western social theorists, who, for the past 200 hundred years, have been in critical engagement on issues that modernists have deemed relevant and significant. However, their voices have not been heard, and it is high time, given the current intercivilizational phase of globalization, that we pay systematic attention to all subjugated voices more earnestly. As an example we could mention the problem of "Conscience," which is of great significance both within the disciplinary frame of reference and the primordial school of social theory as represented by Allama Jafari. The question of "Conscience" in the human sciences can be used as a prime example for future comparative studies that are not necessarily confined to one single problematique but could envelope various dimensions of sociological importance.

Modern thought tends toward not only history but a historicized set of rational/sensual values that hamper our understanding of perennial questions or even the possibility of reflecting on eternal questions that could have eschatological significance for the perfection of self and society in relation to grand metaphysical concerns about which all world religions are concerned. This historicized frame of philosophizing and theorizing has disabled the modern disciplinary human sciences with regard to the question of "Conscience," which is posed as an extra-cultural as well as perennial quest within the realm of reality which is considered as the human universe.

In other words, the secular founders of modernity conceptualized "Conscience" within the framework of the established society, which resulted in an understanding of the human sciences as a handmaiden of capitalist or socialist, nationalist or liberalist, and various context-bounden ideologies that questioned the legitimacy or even the possibility of the universal nature of human personality with conscience at its centre, which is what Allama Jafari considered the right approach. The primacy of conscience as a universal human faculty is not a valid axiom within the frame of disciplinary human sciences as what is of crucial significance within the disciplinary discourse is the dominant cultural values that are devoid of transcendence or revealed canonical considerations. To put it otherwise, conscience as the voice of Transcendence within the cordial dimension of man has turned into a colossal imagined entity called the "conscience collective" that is historicized and self-regulated and not anchored in any celestial or transcendental prophetic tradition. There is no distinct debate on the question of conscience within human sciences, since it is not relevant to think of it as an intellectually separate category, but the best one can do is to fathom it as Leibniz did, namely as a moral force or an emotional reaction to felt guilt or injustice and joy of the mind because of hope for eternal blessedness. It is quite another issue that even this minimal Leibnizian concern with the question of conscience was initially neglected and, finally, within disciplinary human sciences forgotten.

The main critique of Allama Jafari is that this is not only a moral upsurge but a daunting potentiality within the human soul, which could function as a discerning faculty along other faculties that we have at our disposal, such as the heart, mind, hearing, and so on. However, it should be mentioned that the derivative activities of conscience, such as "consciousness," "unconsciousness," "perception," and "self-consciousness," are considered within human sciences but within a historicized paradigm that disables us from fathoming a perennial core character for the human person above all cultures, civilizations, traditions, religions, ethnicities, races, nationalities, and ideologies, which are all dependent upon that universal core that makes the image of man recognizable eternally and enables the possibility of recognizing the humanity of the other even when the other is as different as possible. For Allama Jafari, the question of conscience is a very relevant one, and its unduly neglected importance within disciplinary human sciences is of great significance as is its prime role within the constitution of self, society, and the global world. As alluded to earlier, the disciplinary human sciences and philosophy are not devoid of debates on "conscience," but the very fundamental textures of conscience within this disciplinary frame of reference differ profoundly from what Allama Jafari considers as the most significant aspect of human personality, which is but a reflection of conscience. The disciplinary approach to issues of values, virtues, vices, sins (although this is almost a forgotten dimension within value-neutral disciplinary sciences; nevertheless, there are moral philosophers who still pay some attention within academia to this dimension, too), and morality starts from what is called the "social," and the idea of "conscience" turns into a matter of an external force, which is considered by Durkheim as a reflection of the "collective conscience," namely a common social bond that is expressed by the ideas values, norms, beliefs, and ideologies of the culture, institutionalized in the social structure, and internalized by individual members of that culture. Today, the "collective conscience" of Durkheim would be termed social integration, because the concern is with how units of a social system are coordinated. What Durkheim was denoting with the concept of "collective conscience" is the fact that man has no inner compass in the theological-philosophical-metaphysical-transcendental-religious sense, but adopts forms and contents from society and internalizes what he receives from the surroundings. But, the quality or direction of this shared mentality is not of any significance for Durkheim as long as there is something to share and be like-minded. This is where Allama Jafari's approach to the question of "conscience" could prove intercivilizationally constructive and interdisciplinary heuristic.

For Allama Jafari, the conscience is not a collection of unknown social forces that collectively work for social integration in the face of anomic tendencies, as disciplinary sociology claims. On the contrary, it has a distinctive individual seat that addresses the human person primarily and then has communal/external/cosmic/universal consequences, but the individual element is of utmost significance and cannot be ignored, as its neglect could cost the very existence of the activity of human conscience, as Allama Jafari understands it. The conscience is not only a historical phenomenon that could be historicized and ascribed to a definite social context in a past social fabric, such as Feudalism or Iron Age. The conscience has specific activities and unique concerns to be involved with within Allama Jafari's philosophical paradigm. Besides, it should be mentioned that it has a profound metaphysical character, but this metaphysicality should not hinder us from reflecting upon its nature, character, role, place, and importance within the overall system of perception of reality by the human agent. The conscience is like a distinct faculty within the cosmos of the human self, with various interior textures and levels of intensities depending on the ego's engagement with reality in its transcendence and immanence or how deep the extreme finite has come to be in interaction with the tremendous infinite. It is not impossible to discern its activities both in relation to inner dimensions and interpersonal as well as social and global realms. The health, potency, capability, and dynamism of all other human faculties are dependent upon the level of cultivation one assigns to it. At its highest, it could reflect the divine reality within and about us, and at its lowest, it could hold us morally responsible for the misdeeds we may commit towards ourselves, others, and God. The conscience is where one holds dialogue with oneself. It displays the reality of things (in relation to "I," and how "I" is related to others and the entire gamut of realities outside and within oneself) without any distortion. It has a prescriptive role as well as a guiding role in demonstrating to us that this reality we call life is not meaningless but a deeply meaning-laden project. It could demonstrate the two extreme faces of reality of human person in his best and his worst, namely the conscientious and the un-conscientious self. One of the main reasons we have not thought through the question of conscience within modern disciplinary discourses is the nature of this faculty, which goes beyond the simple understanding of what constitutes the central problems of science, as it has deep metaphysical overtones. However, this question is not essentially different from other essential questions, such as the reality of law, time, space, matter, motion, and energy, as they all escape strictly positivistic conceptualizations. But the intellectual community does not abandon these aforementioned questions due to their metaphysical characteristics. On the contrary, it would be impossible to do science without these notions in some form of practical and operational understanding. The question of conscience is no exception in this regard, and its disappearance from the pantheon of human science discourses cannot be justified in accordance with ideals of modern, secular, disciplinary intellectual enterprise.

To talk about Allama is to think of an institution with many departments and faculties or branches, as he wrote almost on all aspects of human sciences, cultural sciences, historical sciences, social theory, theology, philosophy, cosmology, jurisprudence, law, political theory, art and literature, metaphysics, and various relevant perennial questions that concern man in his fourfold relation to God, Self, History, and Nature. Here, in this introductory chapter, we are not about to dissect all aspects of his philosophy or thought, as the main purpose of this chapter is to introduce Allama Jafari to the global intellectual audience as a social theorist who has been wrongly neglected within sociological discourses. As in all introductory work, the best that one can accomplish here is to extract one minor but important aspect of a thinker's social thought and thereafter attempt to explicate it in some detail, which could hopefully shed some light on certain neglected questions within secular disciplinary discourses on human sciences. To achieve this goal, we have looked at the question of "Conscience" within Allama Jafari's frame of analysis and have explored this question with reference to his critique of the secular disciplinary discourse, which, in his view, has been neglectful towards such a lofty dimension. This also aims at substantiating our claim that the absence of non-secular intellectuals within the canon of human sciences is detrimental to the emergence of global consciousness and intercivilizational dialogue. Of course, in upcoming chapters, we have looked at other aspects of his social thought in relation to sociological tradition in detail.

One of the issues that Allama Jafari was critical about was the lack of intellectual debate on the question of conscience. He narrates an incident while he was at a conference in Europe when he was discussing with a psychologist the importance of conscience and asked about the lack of essential research on this issue among the works of disciplinary psychologists. Surprisingly, the psychologist argued that the reason was very obvious. To delve into such a delicate issue, he said, could be dangerous for the well-being of the individual's health (Jafari, 1381). Allama Jafari time and again argues that the importance of conscience, "has been forgotten within modern philosophical and social theoretical discourses, and one needs to reintroduce this eminent aspect into life" (Jafari 1381, 15).

But Jafari is a philosopher par excellence as he looks for "demonstrable reasons" and rejects any debate that lacks intellectual theorems and convincing reasons. To avoid any logical pitfalls, he looks at the current state of debates from his own point of departure and finds that the question is a worthy problematique and has been erroneously neglected. As he put it, to be able to reintroduce this "excellent dimension into human life anew we need to corroborate the place of man in the scheme of things, which has been reduced by secular thinkers to a link within an unknown chain of things. In other words, we need to reassume a core sense of personality for man" (Jafari 1381, 15).

As he writes for a modern audience, Allama Jafari is not negligent about the question of methodology. He attempts to demonstrate the foundations of his approach and displays in earnest how he has approached the question. His methodology, he states, is "composed of two parts: 1) introspection, and 2) indirect introspective results that we receive from the research of grand thinkers, such as Avecinna, Mulla Sadra, Suhreverdi, Rumi, Attar, Shakespeare, Khalil Gibran, Victor Hugo, Balzac, Tolstoy and so on" (Jafari 1381, 16).

The question of human personality is of great significance for Allama Jafari, and one can locate resemblances with regard to this problematique with the following four Western (not necessarily disciplinary) trends:

1. Humanistic Psychology, which is mainly represented by intellectuals such as G. W. Allport, W. Bridges, J. F. T. Bugental, A. Ellis, E. Fromm, E. Gendlin, J. Gibb, S. Jourard, R. Lowry, A. H. Maslow, C. Moustakas, F. Perls, W. Reich, C. R. Rogers, V. Satir, W. C. Schutz, and A. Wheelis.
2. Existential Philosophy, which one may find among the writings of authors such as J. H. van den Berg, M. Buber, Albert Camus, V. Frankl, A. Georgi, M. Heidegger, R. D. Laing, R. May, J. Ortega y Gasset, D. E. Polkinghorne, P. Ricoeur, J-P. Sartre, S. Strasser, P. Tillich, I. Yalom, R. J. Valle R. J. & M. King, and C. Wilson.
3. Transpersonal Psychology, which is best represented by thinkers such as R. Assagioli, F. Capra, M. Ferguson, S. Grof, M. Micheal T. Roszak, A. K. Kanner, W. Van Dusen, R. Walsh, F. Vaughn, A. Watts, and K. Wilber.
4. Archetypal and Imaginal Psychology, which is best expressed in the writings of J. S. Bolen, J. Hillman, C. G. Jung, T. Moore, E. Neumann, R. Romanyshyn, and R. Sardello.

## HUMANISTIC SOCIAL THEORY

Humanistic psychology is a psychological perspective that emphasizes the study of the whole person. Humanistic psychologists look at human behavior, not only through the eyes of the observer but also through the eyes of the person doing the behaving. Humanistic psychologists believe that an individual's behavior is connected to his inner feelings and self-image. Unlike the behaviorists, humanistic psychologists believe that humans are not solely the product of their environment. Rather, humanistic psychologists study human meanings, understandings, and experiences involved in growing, teaching, and learning. They emphasize characteristics that are shared by all human beings, such as love, grief, caring, and self-worth.

Humanistic psychologists study how people are influenced by their self-perceptions and the personal meanings attached to their experiences. They are not primarily concerned with instinctual drives, responses to external stimuli, or past experiences. Rather, they consider conscious choices, responses to internal needs, and current circumstances to be important in shaping human behavior. They study the mechanisms of human thought. They focus on the structure and organization of what a person knows and how his thoughts, beliefs, expectations and interpretations affect behavior. Humanistic psychologists believe the concept of the "self" held by an individual influences his behavior and is related to his emotional state, well-being, and judgment.

According to humanistic psychologists, the self can be viewed as a schema or organized body of propositions and descriptions that guides the selection and interpretation of new information. The schema is a template against which information is compared. The information can be interpreted to fit a person's schema. Self-schemas act upon information and construct and transform it to be meaningful to the self.

## EXISTENTIAL SOCIAL THEORY

"Authentic Existence" is a technical expression within existential philosophy and psychology. An "authentic" person is one who has a clear sense of his or her purpose in life. Within this position, the consciousness is considered as a principal source of meaning. Existentialism understands the human to be challenged by the reality of temporary existence and argues that life has no inherent meaning. Instead, it claims, meaning has to be constructed. Authentic human beings, it claims, are those who can face existential futility and yet still go on to construct a meaningful life. Existentialism represents the philosophical root of the phenomenological approach to personality.

After WWII, this philosophy gained a large following in Europe. The purpose of existential philosophy was to regain contact with the experiences of being ALIVE and AWARE. Key questions of existential philosophy are: What is the nature of existence? How does it feel? What does it mean?

The key issue for existential psychology is as follows: All existence ends in death. Therefore, what is the point? The human challenge is this: Do we descend into nothingness or do we have the "courage to be"? All we have is existence, so existential psychology is about helping people to BE and take responsibility for their lives.

According to the existentialists (philosophers, sociologists, or psychologists), human beings have no existence apart from the world. Being-in-the-world or *dasein* IS man's existence. *Dasein* is the whole of mankind's existence. The basic issue in life is that life inevitably ends in death. Thus, we experience angst or anguish because of our awareness of death's inevitability. So, we either retreat into nothingness or have the courage to BE. The extreme of the retreat into nothingness is suicide, but we can also retreat into nothingness by not living authentic lives.

From this perspective it is extremely important that we "BE," i.e., that we live authentically. This entails living a life that is honest, insightful, and morally correct. Authenticity is about living genuinely with one's angst and achieving meaning despite the temporary nature of one's existence. Life has no meaning unless one creates it. Friedrich Nietzsche said that the only logical response to this void and meaninglessness was to rise above it and become a "superman."

We are all responsible for our choices, but even honest choices will not always be good ones. One will still feel guilty about failing to fulfill all the possibilities in one's life. Existential guilt, or existential anxiety or angst, is inescapable. The existential approach also has much more negative undertones than the humanistic approach. It emphasizes powerlessness, loneliness, emptiness, and angst, and admits that it is very hard to find meaning and value in our lives.

## TRANSPERSONAL SOCIAL THEORY

Transpersonal psychology is the field of psychology that integrates psychological concepts, theories, and methods with the subject matter and practices of the spiritual disciplines. It uses both quantitative and qualitative methods; its central concepts are nonduality, self-transcendence, optimal human development, and mental health; and its core practices include meditation and ritual. Transpersonal psychologists' interests include the assessment, characteristics, antecedents, and consequences of spiritual and self-transcendent experiences, mystical states of consciousness, mindfulness and meditative practices, and shamanic states. Transpersonal psychologists are also interested in the embodiment and integration of these states into everyday life, as well as in the overlap of spiritual experiences with disturbed states, such as psychosis and depression, the assessment and promotion of transpersonal characteristics in individuals, and the transpersonal dimensions of interpersonal relationships, community, service, and encounters with the natural world.

Transpersonal psychology is based on *non-duality*, the recognition that each part (e.g., each person) is fundamentally and ultimately a part of the whole (the cosmos). This view is radically different from psychological approaches founded on the premises of mechanism, atomism, reductionism, and separateness. From this insight come two other central insights: the *intrinsic health* and basic goodness of the whole and each of its parts, and the validity of *self-transcendence* from the conditional and conditioned personality to a sense of identity, which is deeper, broader, and more unified with the whole.

The root of the term transpersonal, or "beyond the personal," reflects this impulse towards that which is more universal than individual identity. The root of the word "personal" comes from *persona* or the masks worn by Greek actors to portray characters, so the transpersonal could literally mean "beyond the mask." These masks both hide the actor and reveal the actor's role. Following this metaphor, transpersonal psychology seeks to disclose and develop the source and deeper nature of identity, being, and ground. It is important to note that non-duality and self-transcendence do not negate the importance of embodiment, individuality, and personalness. Transpersonal psychology's orientation is inclusive, valuing and integrating the following: psychological and spiritual development; the personal and the transpersonal; exceptional mental health, ordinary experience, and states of suffering; ordinary and extraordinary states of consciousness; the transpersonal aspects of modern Western perspectives, Eastern wisdom traditions, (some) postmodern insights, and many indigenous traditions; and analytical intellect and contemplative ways of knowing. For example, the integral approach continues to advance the articulation of this inclusive view, maintaining both the validity and the limitations of various psychological approaches.

Transpersonal psychology is a field of inquiry that includes theory, research, and practice, offering insights based on research, experience, and practices for evaluating and confirming or disconfirming its findings. It is scientific in the broad sense of the phenomenological or human sciences, including, but not being limited to, positivistic approaches. Overlaps between psychology and spirituality have been present in both psychology (e.g.,

James, Jung, and Maslow) and the spiritual traditions (which have their own rich views of development, cognition, social interactions, suffering, and healing). Transpersonal psychology has highlighted this overlap, allowing further development of theory and application.

Transpersonal psychology has benefits for both psychology and the spiritual disciplines. Psychology can expand toward a fuller and richer accounting of the complete range of experience and human potential, incorporating practices that speak more directly and completely to the depth of human nature. The spiritual disciplines can integrate insights and skills about human development, emotional healing, and psychological growth to deal more skillfully with various impediments to spiritual development, such as resistance to change and transformation, unresolved childhood traumas and abuse, the inner critic or superego as it appears on the spiritual journey, and spiritual awakening, which is so disintegrating and difficult that it becomes a spiritual emergency. Spiritual traditions can use these issues as gateways, rather than obstacles, to self-realization.

According to transpersonal psychology, human growth occurs beyond the scope and limitations of personality, and moves on to larger realms of consciousness. The transpersonal view acknowledges the possibility and potential of all human beings to achieve states that traditionally have been ascribed exclusively to eastern yogis and mystics, and includes the study of experiences and processes in man that Western science just recently has begun to explore. Within the spiritual teachings of the East and traditional medicine practices, these states have been known for thousands of years and thoroughly examined, such as psycho-spiritual growth and transformation by awakening and expressions of *kundalini* in Hindu practice, charts of the *chakra*s, the subtle energy centers in yogic techniques, and the science of Chi, the universal life force in traditional Chinese medicine.

Historically and traditionally, Western psychology and psychiatry have focused exclusively on pathological features of the human mind, and rejected all forms of altered states of consciousness, spiritual experiences, and processes as abnormal and undesirable. The field of transpersonal psychology is set once again on including the spiritual realm in Western science, and regards such processes and experiences as basically natural and positive.

## ARCHETYPAL AND IMAGINAL SOCIAL THEORY

The central aim of this theory is the development of the soul through the cultivation of imaginal life in the personal, cultural, and transpersonal domains. This approach derives from existential-phenomenology and archetypal psychology.

It also echoes themes expressed by humanistic psychologists over the past four decades, initiated by the work of Carl Rogers and Abraham Maslow and other archetypal or imaginal psychologists who have made strong arguments for the creative potential and role of human personality in the evolution of human existence. However, it is the impact of James Hillman's archetypal psychology that brought back the question of soul to psychology. But as "imaginal" psychology, it cannot truly overcome psychology's positivistic, personalistic bias that it set out to overcome. In rectifying this heuristic problem, the proponents of this position need to reevaluate the roles of metaphysics, myths, poetics, music, as well as axiomatic dimensions within modernity, as the disciplinary social sciences seem to be oblivious about the questions of "belongingness" and "connection." Archetypal and imaginal psychology, on the other hand, evokes the vision of belongingness and connection. It provides a framework for imagining a profound intimacy between ourselves and our world in ways that mainstream psychology does not address. First, archetypal and imaginal psychology functions within a larger meta-story in which every human being is an integral part of a living cosmos. This organismic view allows for the possibility of communication between the living whole and its parts in a way that a lifeless clockwork universe cannot. Second, archetypal clients tend to be imagined in less pathological ways than in traditional clinical perspectives. The use of archetypal symbolism provides glimpses into the complexities of human personality and considers a wide range of human expression as acceptable. Psychopathology is less a label than an excessive or inhibited aspect of natural functioning. Third, as all people are constellated from a finite pool of elements uniquely configured in the birth chart, a person can preserve a sense of individuality without feeling alienated from the larger human community. Fourth, archetypal and imaginal psychology suggests that a client's situation is not simply the result of random and chaotic processes. The whole of the archetypal perspective reflects a world that is orderly and potentially understandable. This can help return to a client a sense of control in life, a sense that his own developmental process includes the apparent chaos as a part of his larger life pattern. Because life may feel out of our control, it does not mean that it is actually out of control. Larger guiding factors may occasionally wreak havoc with the ego's plans, challenging us to maintain a certain fluidity and adaptability to life's ever-turning circumstances. This flexibility is necessary for the survival of the fittest, as those who best adapt to fit into the changing environment tend to thrive.

In each of these trends, one can see the paradigmatic concern with the centrality of the human ego within the scheme of things that has somehow been denied since the inception of the contemporary world-system. However, these trends do not take the centrality of human personality as an indicator of what Allama Jafari considers as conscience, which is capable of organizing and guiding of grand psycho-socio-cosmic tasks. Yet, it is important to realize that there are possibilities between these occidentalistic trends and Allama Jafari's concern about the human personality and conscience as its core. As he argues, until one does not "not recognize the importance of ideal 'personality' for himself as a cornerstone of the desired 'I,' it is impossible to attain the heights of conscience as the seat of the 'inner voice' towards morality" (Jafari 1381, 22).

One of the main factors that makes for metaphysical compatibilities between Allama Jafari's and the above-mentioned occidentalist trends to be complex (if not impossible) is the question of religious worldview, which envelops the entire discourse of Allama Jafari's reflection upon human existence. For him life is "another name for being present before the Divine. If 'I,' for whatever reason, is unable or unwilling to stand before the Divine as a receiver of the grace, he or she would not realize the authentic identity of himself or herself" (Jafari 1381, 33).

Having said that, one should recall that with the aforementioned trends one can discern a religious position along the secular, transcendental, and spiritual ones, too, namely the position represented by Jewish and Christian philosophers such as Buber and Tillich. These resemblances, similarities and convergences could be of great intercivilizational significance in furthering the question along new frontiers, which could enable us in our efforts to establish a global ethics based on sound and authentic grounds.

An ethic devoid of sound and authentic grounds would not lead us to moral coexistence, since the grounds such as trade, finance and politics, when devoid of this authentic dimension, will present themselves as problems rather than solutions. Allama Jafari's sociohistorical analysis and philosophical search led him to believe that "man has an innate ability like a compass to find the pole, but societies and cultures decide what the pole is for the majority" (Jafari 1381, 66).

In other words, we need to re-establish the importance of innate ideas within human sciences by re-evaluating the place of evolutionary theories that erroneously put the question of "innateness" in contrast to "evolution" within the contexts of humanities and cultural studies. These two dimensions need not reject one another, as both are part and parcel of the primary and secondary dimensions of human reality as best expressed in Iqbalian ego philosophy.

When searching for the building-blocks of a global ethics, we should not only look at what are conventionally called "cultures," since we can witness the emergence of a global civic culture in our time, namely a culture that contains further elements such as the idea of human rights, the principles of democratic legitimacy and public accountability, the emerging ethos of evidence

and proof, the ideals and purposes of the United Nations, and the consciousness of a shared earthly ecosystem, which shape expectations throughout the
world. These are significant manifestations of this world culture. Nevertheless,
the indispensable principle of a global ethics needs a much deeper grounding
than what the contemporary proponents of global ethics have been arguing for.
For Allama Jafari, this "indispensable principle" is the "conscience." In fact,
he argues that the only faculty "which can bring us as human beings together
and invite us to a life of harmony by establishing true and logical coexistence
is 'Conscience'" (Jafari 1381, 78).

The main aim of global ethicists is coexistence on a large scale. This cannot be achieved if peace is not secured by every individual person within
himself or herself. To achieve true peace in all its dimensions, it must first
be admitted that man has a core and that this core is innate and not forced
upon him from without. Allama Jafari puts this idea in the following fashion:
"Anyone who is able to harmonize the inner and outer motives of the self
will be able to live a rational life that is not swayed by the ebbs and flows of
passions. What is able to make this harmony become a reality is what we call
'Human Personality'" (Jafari 1381, 81).

For Allama Jafari, "Conscience" or "Vijdan" is capable of bringing about
the norms and guiding principles of normative discourses, which may be of
great significance in the regeneration of global ethics. But the conscience, he
says, "like all other aspects of reality, has degrees and layers, and the highest level of conscience, i.e., . . . 'Noble Conscience,' can be brought about
through cultivation, abstention of carnal desires, and endurance in the face of
difficulties" (Jafari 1381, 250).

It is not difficult to realize that Allama Jafari's emphasis on the individual's
role within the scheme of things may come into collision with many disciplinary discourses on the human self. It is not surprising, therefore, that within
disciplinary discourses there is no essential debate on "conscience"—and this
is exactly the point that Allama Jafari, like the aforementioned four groups
of thinkers, attempts to make clear. Although he agrees that the emerging
global civic culture seems to give rise to new normative elements, nevertheless he questions the guiding principles of these "normative elements" and as
inquires of what this normativity consists.

As Allama Jafari remarks, the difficulty in fathoming the importance of
conscience is due to the role of metaphysics in discerning its scope and depth
within the parameters of contemporary modernist social theory, which has
turned away from metaphysical contemplations. But, this is too bad for modernist secular thinking, and this lack should not be pardoned or be considered
as a point of strength, as questions that burden the soul need to be answered.
By ignoring them, we cannot resolve the agony of the soul. To separate

thought from existence, we cannot bring about creativity (in the sense that is related to the Creator) but rather illusion that is devoid of redemption. Metaphysics is the science that distinguishes between imagination/creativity and illusion, and brings existential clarity with regard to our thinking process. However, when we divorce the process of thinking and existence conceptually, and consider these distinctions existentially valid, we end up in the land of illusion, as we are today. In *The Secular City*, Harvey Cox asserted that "the era of metaphysics is dead," and that "politics replaces metaphysics as the language of theology" (Cox 1968, 22). Perhaps metaphysics is dead for Cox, who apparently subscribes to the doctrine of God's hiddenness. But, obviously, it is very much alive for Altizer, for Bishop Robinson, for B-psychology, for the Eastern and Perennial and Primordial social thinkers. It seems that thinkers such as Cox may have completely misread the signs of the times, for it appears far more likely that we are witnessing today a significant rebirth of metaphysics. Additionally, the upsurge of existential and neurotic anxieties demonstrate clearly that the soul of humanity is in need of communion with the Holy, and no science can address the intellectual soul of men better than metaphysics. Even contemporary social sciences—such as sociology, social psychology and social theory—are now asking ultimate ontological questions about the nature of Being. Perhaps it was inevitable that social theory should do this. As Tillich has indicated, there are two kinds of anxiety—neurotic and existential—and only ontology can distinguish the one from the other. Neurotic anxiety is unreal, or, rather, has a misplaced object of attention, while existential anxiety is the result of a realistic analysis of the way things actually are. Clearly, it is important to distinguish the two, and that is why Tillich complained about the lack of an ontological analysis of anxiety and a sharp distinction between existential and pathological anxiety. Some decades ago, Jacques Maritain wrote what Allama Jafari also stated in relation to the rediscovery of "Conscience," namely what is essentially needed is a renewal of metaphysics. What is needed, first and foremost, is a rediscovery of "Being," and, by the same token, a rediscovery of love. This means, axiomatically, a rediscovery of God. As he put it, "In perceiving Being, Reason knows God" (Tillich 1932, 34).

This is to argue that the absence of a solid metaphysical debate on the role of conscience within contemporary philosophy and social theory is itself a sign that God is not only a name but also a reality, whose absence from our existence empties not only our symbolic universe but what we call life, too. In not perceiving God, we lose both being and the very core of what we consider as Reason, since the reason of being is deeply intertwined with the being of reason. The one without the other is unthinkable, and those discourses that have presented these three dimensions separately or in contrast to one another have actually extinguished the very voice within us that makes us humane in the form of human beings. In the words of Allama Jafari, "Conscience is the voice of God within us" (Jafari 1381, 308).

I would like to end this introductory chapter on Allama Jafari's views on the pivotal significance of inner life with the following quote from Henry David Thoreau, who, in "Walden," contended:

> It is easier to sail many thousand miles through cold and storm and cannibals, in a government ship, with five hundred men and boys to assist one, than it is to explore the private sea, the Atlantic and Pacific Ocean, of one's being alone. (Thoreau 1922, 14)

## Chapter Three

# Human Sciences and the Heptafold Domains of Sociology

In my previous research work, I have problematized the very concept of "Sociology" and how and on what basis we can embrace or refuse an intellectual as a sociologist in the pantheon of the sociological temple. This has been one of my main concerns in studying sociology. There is no doubt that we are faced with a set of definitions that have monopolized the sociological context. This monopolized notion of sociological understanding obstructs the emergence of alternate imaginations within the parameters of social theory. In my previous book, *Sociological Relevance of Primordial School of Social Theory*, I attempted to present the importance of this theory by focusing on Muttahari and Beheshti as two very instrumental social theorists who have been sorely neglected in the global context of sociological theory. In this work, I aim to continue the same line of argument by bringing in another Iranian writer who has worked mainly on questions of significance within the context of the humanities and social sciences without being committed to empiricism, rationalism, positivism, or liberalism. Although it should be admitted that while Mohammad Taghi Jafari (better known as Allama Jafari) is not committed to the aforementioned *isms*, it does not mean that he is against the pivotal role played by empirics, rationality, positivity, and liberty in the constitution of self and society within the parameters of leben.

Nevertheless, we need to reconceptualize the current sociological configuration in a primordial fashion, which, in turn, would enable us to corroborate our problematization of Allama Jafari as a sociologist or social theorist who needs to be taken seriously by the worldwide community of sociologists. In working towards this goal, I have come up with a model, which consists of seven domains: (1) Domain of Social Research, (2) Domain of Sociological Theory, (3) Domain of Social Theory, (4) Domain of Social Philosophy, (5) Domain of Metatheory, (6) Domain of Metaphysics, and (7) Domain of Solitude.

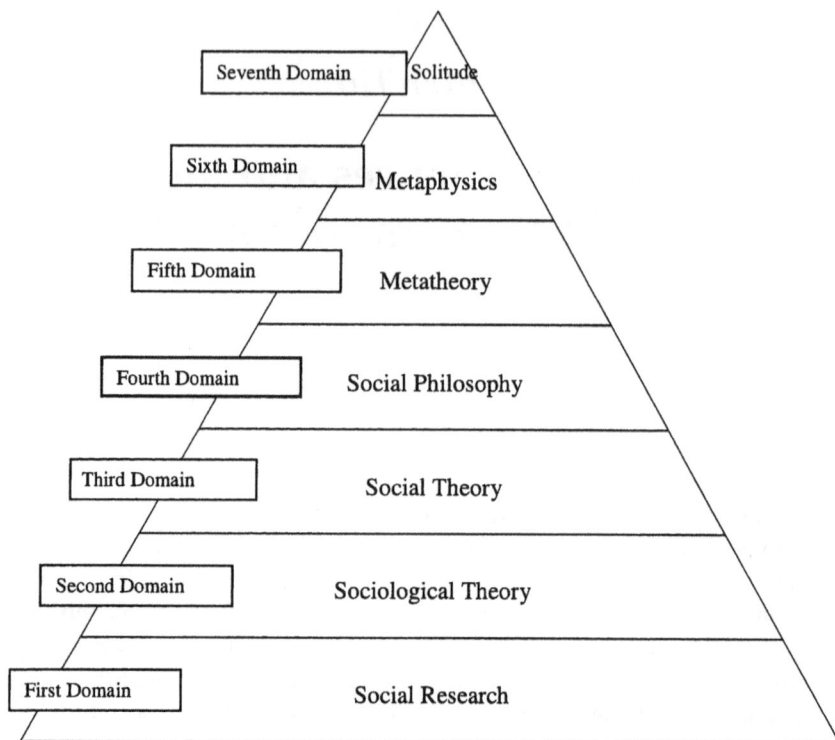

Figure 3.1.  Heptafold domains and the social.

The following is a brief explanation of each of these domains, which will assist readers in having a clearer picture of what we denote by these heptafold dimensions of the sociological imagination.

## DOMAIN OF SOCIAL RESEARCH

By social research, I mean that aspect of social studies where scholars are mainly concerned with methodological issues and where the most significant field of research is considered to be empirical questions that are quantifiable and have no organic connection with rational or intellectual dimensions of existence. In other words, any abstraction is shunned or considered of no analytical value, as both rationalism and extra-rational concerns are viewed suspiciously. In sum, the question of application is the keyword in this domain.

## DOMAIN OF SOCIOLOGICAL THEORY

This domain is where social scientists are conscious about the shortcomings of extreme empiricism, since the very idea of society is not empirically discernible and those who insist on the corroboration of the "Social" on an empirical basis would willy-nilly encounter insurmountable challenges. Thus, scholars have become sharper by taking the dialectical challenges of holism more seriously, and this has led them to pose questions of universal significance while taking the particular critiques into consideration, too. In other words, in this domain, we seem to move a bit higher in the ladder of abstract refinement by expanding the scope of imagination from sensory data to rational data.

## DOMAIN OF SOCIAL THEORY

In this domain, we witness a sea-change where the central question of disciplinary thinking is treated in an undisciplinary fashion. In other words, scholars in this domain work with a more intense abstract sense of theorizing, where compartmentalized approaches to reality are disregarded. Ontologically, the scholars are still married to the ideal of rationalism without moving an inch towards intellectual realms of imagination.

## DOMAIN OF SOCIAL PHILOSOPHY

In this domain, the question of scientific ethos is replaced by a Socratian Ethics. Here the very question of knowledge is treated in an existential fashion, rather than thinking of it in a professional manner that may fall within the parameters of the disciplinarization of science and the compartmentalization of knowledge, or the fragmentalization of being.

## DOMAIN OF METATHEORY

Scholars who work within this domain of intelligible imagination have not yet reached the conclusion that human existence is not only of contingental significance but that permanental dimensions play a vital role in the constitution of self and society. In other words, any study of the "Social" should take these twains very seriously without unduly leaning on any one at the expense of the other. However, scholars who work at this level are conscious about the ultra-rational characters of human life and the importance of extra-rational problems in constituting the very core of rational concepts. Without the admission of this higher field of ontic significance, the very question of rationalism would seem very irrational indeed. In other words, the question of theory at this level is not considered in an analytical fashion but, rather, in a poetical manner, which views the configuration of theory in its pristine sense as a mode of vision, as this is how theory initially was intended to be.

## DOMAIN OF METAPHYSICS

This is the field where all aspects of the reality of human perceptive faculties are embraced in a systematic fashion. That is to say, the sensory, the rational, and the intelligible dimensions are confirmed as part and parcel of human reality. In other words, in conceptualizing the poles of reality, scholars take into consideration both contingency and permanence in relation to empirics, rationality, and intelligibility. We are faced with three different but interrelated conceptual frameworks where concepts are either of empirical origin or rational relevance and intellectual significance. These would surely influence the scope, character, and quality of the imagination, which would be at the disposal of the sociological inquirer. Within this domain, the questions are not only of quantifiable characters, as the reality of human existence can consist of qualitative and spiritual natures. Although here we work with concepts, the quality of our thinking is not concept-driven, as scholars are deeply conscious about the nature of leben, which is unconceptual in its reality. Of course, this entails a very different approach to the very process of conceiving of reality that envelops the human domain, which has been unduly compartmentalized in modernist readings of metaphysics.

## DOMAIN OF SOLITUDE

This concept has been employed by Kierkegaard, Nietzsche, and Dostoevsky in a very technical fashion. It has also been elaborated upon by Ralph Harper within the context of the poetry of nostalgic homelessness of the human spirit. However, this technical interpretation is not what we have in mind. The domain that we have termed the "Seventh Solitude" is best understood as the creative power of the human self, whereby poets compose poems with the same words as ordinary people use in their daily conversations, but in the mind of a poet they turn into beautiful visionary landscapes. This is also the case with geometricians, scientists, artists, philosophers, and mathematicians, who change the way we live in the world through their dreams. Note that these dreams in their initial stages are never conceptual constructions of systematic nature, but to disregard this dimension of human reality or the reality of life is to forget the volcanic possibilities that are at human disposal. In other words, our sociological imagination should not block the influx of this domain into the overall structures of sociology as an intellectual pursuit.

## THE HEPTAFOLD DOMAINS AND THE SOCIAL

Any discourse on the "Social" is concerned with all of these heptafold domains, as shown in Figure 3.1, but what distinguishes different paradigms of sociological analyses is the issue of how these domains relate to each other. In other words, the difference between the disciplinary style of "doing sociology" and the primordial school of social theory is in the manner that these domains are conceptualized of. In the former, what is conceived of as sociology relates mainly to the first, second, and third domains, while connections to the upper domains are either not considered vital or else totally neglected, based on the modernist argument that there are substantial differences between sociology, social philosophy, and metaphysics. Finally, no importance is attached to the Seventh Domain—where intuition, imagination, intellection, extra-sensory inspiration, and extra-rational conceptions play a significant role in the constitution of human reasoning, rationality, intellection, intuition, intelligence, self-understanding, consciousness, self-consciousness, and conscience.

In my reading of Allama Jafari, I have come to conclude that he seems to be moving between all domains of human sciences without neglecting one on behalf of the others. But this does not mean that Allama Jafari's position is strong in all heptafold domains of sociological reasoning, as it is readily discernible that he seems to move on the upper domains of the "sociographic imagination," which is more focused on *metaphors* (i.e., based on analogous reasoning) rather than *diaphors* (i.e., distinctions based on analytical reasoning). But this critique in reverse is applicable to the disciplinary paradigm, too, where academic sociologists seem to move solely in the lower domains of the "sociographic imagination," which is more focused on diaphoric reasoning and devoid of metaphoric imagination.

To argue for diaphoric reasoning over and against metaphoric imagination, or the other way around, or even to prefer to define sociological imagination in terms of "lower domains" at the expense of "upper domains," or otherwise, would not be a good sociological policy for a world that is moving towards more interdependence and unity. We need a sociological model where all of these domains are integrated into a whole, which can be considered as an integral dimension of any theory on humanity.

In my reading of humanities, which is deeply under the tutelage of disciplinary *weltanschauung*, there are very few spaces for novel geometrical approaches to the most urgent question of human sciences, namely self as a social individuated reality composed of innerly externalized dimensions. The facts of human complexities have been ostracized within disciplinary parameters due to different pretexts, but thinkers such as Ali Shariati, Imam Musa Sadr, Taleghani, Beheshti, Muttahari, Iqbal, and Allama Jafari are prominent examples who indicate that the question of the social is as much a diaphoric problem as a metaphoric challenge, which cannot be imagined solely in the diaphoric sense.

In this regard, we can use a comparison that has been employed by Loet Leydesdorff in his analysis of socionomy beyond sociology, where he argues that John Urry's 2000 study enables us to introduce a new set of metaphors into the social sciences. Leydesdorff explains his position by looking at the history of ideas and argues that astronomy emerged during the Scientific Revolution as part of the new (mechanistic) philosophy. Might Urry's orientation towards complex systems theory allow for a next step "beyond sociology." This is to say, he explains, that:

Complex systems theory enables us to introduce a new set of metaphors into the social sciences. However, Urry does not wish to evaluate metaphors in terms of what precisely they help to explain or not, and to what extent. The new metaphors of complex systems theory are used to enrich the description of a set of problems that have been defined from within the tradition of sociology. The metaphors are based on analogies and not elaborated into analytical distinctions that can be entertained as hypotheses. For example, Urry argues that within sociology the structure/action dichotomy (Giddens, Habermas, Münch, and others) can be abandoned on the basis of the insights of complex systems theory. Change does not necessarily refer to (human) agency, because structures can change endogenously as a result of interactions among fluxes. However, this insight is not further discussed analytically: networks can only change endogenously if there are imbalances at interfaces that lead to interactions and disturbances. The network analyst would like to know why these imbalances emerged, how they are generated, and under what conditions they can be reproduced. This type of questioning would require a mathematical conceptualization of the subject under study (e.g., in terms of eigenvector and frequency analyses) that Urry avoids. Instead, the author replaces the methodological dichotomy of structure and action (Giddens 1979, 14) with the epistemological one of humans and non-humans, as in "actor-network theory." In "actor-network theory" technologies can impose their own agency on the world based on previous investments ("stabilizations") in them. Should one then not distinguish between social networks of reflexive communications that are able to provide instantaneous meaning to these technologies (by rewriting their meaning), and heterogeneous networks (including non-humans) which have been stabilized in historical time (and are therefore potentially available to be rewritten)? In actor-network theory, "humans" are black-boxed as "actants" taking part in the networks in a mode similar to non-humans. Their specific capacity for constructing instantaneous time both individually (that is, psychologically) and through the use of communication (e.g., ICT) is not addressed. How are "humans" related to the networks in which they relate? Are they related as bodies, as psyches, or as social representations? Urry mentions that humans can also be important in a network by being absent. Does one always need the human body, or can one sometimes consider only the representation that covers the file? A medical doctor may need the body for physical examination, but does the other person need to be physically present in a scientific discussion? How can "humans" be represented differently as bodies, as agencies that provide meaning, and in interactions among systems of communication? The shift towards a socionomy would require not only a different vocabulary, but also a further abstraction of the subject of sociological analysis. The social network does not exist in real life like a biological system, but it develops evolutionarily. Society contains a cultural dynamics with the characteristics of another evolution. The complex system of social coordination is instantiated in the events that happen to occur, but which could have been otherwise. In other words, the social system can be analyzed in terms of a phase space of possible configurations, while the observable states inform us about the trajectories of the system that happened as events in the state space. The selection mechanisms, however, cannot be retrieved inductively from the positive instances. The instantiations inform us about these mechanisms by translating the observations into discourses. The hypothesis of a "missing link," for example, assumes the specification of an *ex ante* expectation already at the level of biology. The analysis of cultural evolution, however, has first to specify an equivalent of "natural selection." Can the biological metaphor be used for the sociological distinction? What are the selection mechanisms of cultural evolution, and how do they operate when producing the social phenomena that can be observed? One does not expect a single selecting mechanism to operate in society. Markets select, but other selective mechanisms are simultaneously at work. Neither markets nor other selection mechanisms can be considered as biologically given. Markets can be internally differentiated (e.g., in terms of labour markets, consumer markets, etc.), and the various dynamics compete as mechanisms of social coordination. All these mechanisms (e.g., markets, legal systems, etc.) have historically been constructed, but once in place they may increasingly begin to feedback as selectors on the variations produced historically and provided by the other subsystems. Cultural evolution proceeds under the selection pressure of all the subsystems of the social system upon one another. The positive instances can inform our hypotheses concerning the question of these selections, but only on the condition that the selection mechanisms have first been specified. The model of a socionomy is hypothetico-deductive because the selection mechanisms cannot be induced on the basis of the observable "facts." The latter provide us only with the observable variation. (Leydesdorff 2002).

The same sort of argument could be used in regard to the primordial configuration of sociological understanding. In other words, the shift towards a primordial sociology would require not only a different vocabulary, but also a further abstraction of the subject of sociological analysis. This metaphoric shift is amazingly discernible in the Jafarian frame of reference, which is of profound sociographical significance, but as yet the ground has not been tilled by sociologists around the globe. We could paraphrase what Urry and Leydesdorff argue in terms of network discourses by applying it to Allama Jafari's sociological universe, which seems to unite all domains of social significance within the body of his sociological theory. Of course, there are many undertheorized grounds that need to be reconstructed, and Allama Jafari himself confessed (Jafari 1387, 145) to various shortcomings which one may come across within his theoretical paradigm, which we have termed as primordial school of social theory. The model we have provided in previous pages is an attempt to highlight the possibility of the "pendulum abstracting move," which we, as sociologists, need to practice more often, both within existing disciplines as well as imaginatively. This is to argue that we need to unlearn the conventional modes of thinking in unidimensional fashion, which, for instance, seems to put aesthetics over accuracy or the latter in opposition to other aspects of reality, such as the modernist quarrel of quality versus quantity. Jafari seems to be opening a new chapter in sociographical imagination, which is deeply needed within the contemporary balkanized world of value systems. Of course, this approach is immensely untheorized, and the founding patrons or matrons of the primordial school of social theory are sadly unknown within leading discourses on social sciences, humanities, and cultural studies around the globe.

*Chapter Four*

# Human Sciences in the
# Past, Present, and Future

One of the most significant issues within the social sciences is the question of research and its position within the sociological paradigm, both historically and contemporarily. Allama Jafari focused on this issue at Sheffield University in 1995. In conceptualizing this problematique, he believes that we need to concentrate on three periods of time, i.e., Past, Present, and Future of the human sciences in relation to the position of the humanities, which needs to be strengthened in the light of research. In this regard, Jafari proposed four issues, which are of significance in terms of humanities:

1. The special position of human sciences vis-à-vis technology in its general sense.
2. The particular place of humanities among other branches of knowledge and sciences in a general sense.
3. The normative position of social sciences vis-à-vis other branches of knowledge and industry.
4. Who does research in the humanities, and under what conditions. (Jafari 1995, 207)

## HUMAN SCIENCES REVISITED

One of the most contentious issues within the humanities is how to define human sciences and, by extension, what to consider as important questions within the parameters of the humanities. Jeffrey C. Alexander, one of the early pioneers in this regard, has dared to approach the questions of the importance of the humanities and the issues of human importance, both of which are of great relevance within the context of sociology. Allama Jafari is conscious about these issues and has paid profound attention to the problem of definition (and of how to draw the borders of human sciences) in his work the *Message of Wisdom*.

In defining human sciences, Jafari takes the primary part (i.e., human) very seriously by arguing that "Our definition of human sciences consists of a great many issues and principles where the human being lies at the centre of these problematiques" (Jafari 1386, 211).

Since the central problem of humanities is the question of the human self or the human personality, Allama Jafari divides the human sciences into seven different fields based on their respective distance from the overarching problematique, i.e., the human being or the personality of the human self. He further argues that

> apart from behavioralists within the human sciences, who reduce the spirit of human being to stimulus, it is undeniable that humanities are directly or indirectly concerned with the self of the human person in the sense of how to revitalize the diverse dimensions of the human being in an integral fashion. . . . Of course, it should be reemphasized that sociologists employ different concepts in denoting the central issue of human sciences, such as *personality*, *spirit* and *soul*. (Jafari 1386, 213)

In Jafari's view, human sciences would lose its *raison d'etre* if, as he puts it, "social scientists continue neglecting to consider the pivotal role of *self* in the constitution of the human person" (213).

In other words, in neglecting the crucial position of the self in the constitution of human person within the context of the human sciences, sociologists have tended gradually to replace the "essence" by "appearance." To put it differently, as Allama Jafari says,

> once we overlook the importance of character in the constitution of the human self this would set in the beginning of a trend which shall lead finally in marginalizing of reasons by effects and statistics by pivotal conditions. However, it should be borne in mind that this reductionist approach did not settle at this stage but has gone further by neglecting these phenomena and effects . . . and, instead, focusing on behaviors. . . . Disregarding the essential role of the self in the constitution of human life both individually and collectively has led to five mistaken assumptions which need to be discussed in detail. (Jafari 1386, 213)

Jafari has indentified five cardinal sins in the context of disciplinary social thought. They can be classified as follows:

1. Activities and phenomena such as emotions, thought, intelligence, imagination, will, freedom, and various values have been conceptualized within

disciplinary social sciences without assigning any essential role for the "self" as an organizing principle in the sustenance of the aforementioned abilities within the human person. In other words, by overlooking the importance of the "self," disciplinary sociologists have gradually lost the unifying principle of human sciences. Further, these disparaged aspects which were studied as relevant issues within human sciences finally got relegated to the margins. . . . By following Hume, who denied the universals, the human self (as a substantial permanent unifying principle in the human person), causality and the impossibility of inferring ought-to-be from is-ness, the disciplinary paradigms fell into the habit of ever-reducing the higher levels to lower levels.

2. Paradigmatic values, such as Ethics, Gnosis, and Life-affirming religion, which are embedded potentially in the heart of the "human consciousness" and human life itself would lose its humanity and vitality without the presence of this crucial essence and disappear altogether from the context of the disciplinary social sciences. Doubtless this led to the catastrophic loss of unifying principle of human sciences, which is the recognition of the I-ness as the central problem of humanities.

3. To deny the executive significance of self as a governing principle in the human sciences has led to negligence of possibility of realization of human personality through virtues, sense of duty, and acting regardless of utilitarian gain.

4. The sense of liberty, which is one of the grandest privileges of human beings that could be employed in the course of life, is impossible to be realized as a faculty without the supervision and sovereignty of "I" before the spectrums of virtues and vices.

5. By deauthoring the authorial dimension of human self in the context of humanities, disciplinary sociology has caused a sense of emptiness, which is best termed as alienating state of being. That is very much evident in the contemporary society. Despite material progress in modernist culture, the modern self is suffering from nihilism, but these nihilistic tendencies are disguised under the beautiful motto of "rule of law" in advanced industrial societies. (Jafari 1386, 213–15)

Before entering the universe of Jafari's social thought, we need to find out what "style" of sociology he was elaborating or what kind of social theory on which his social thought was focused. We could think of three styles of narratives within a sociological context—descriptive, explanatory, and normative. Of course, it is doubtless that the best theories are those that encompass all the three levels of narrativity. Besides, an ideal sociologist is one who can work in all seven domains without being bounded to any

specific domain. However, the style by which Jafari could be best understood is a normative approach of theorizing with an imaginative kind of
explanatory model that enjoys non-disciplinary descriptive modality in
illustrating social issues.

In other words, the anchorage of Jafari's theorizing project is on the normative conception of society, where the abyss between *is* and *ought-to* should
not be conceived of as inseparable, because the heart of community is the human self that oscillates between the actual and the ideal incessantly. In other
words, when thinking of human sciences and their place in human societies
across the globe, we should realize that, as Allama Jafari says,

> the state of humanities as it "is" and as it "ought to be," is based on the assump-
> tion that human sciences are concerned with the leben of human being, whose
> being consists of two inseparable domains of "is" and "ought-to-be." In other
> words, the disciplinary paradigms within the human sciences have lost contact
> with this profound dimension of human life, which is an eternal expression of
> the spirit of human self. Losing this connection is tantamount to succumbing
> before the instrumentalist approach to life, which would reduce the being of
> humanity into a reified thing. The only way forward in rescuing human sciences,
> which is another word for redeeming humanity, as they both are in a reciprocal
> relationship, is to realize the normative possibilities within the human self which
> are "present" but in need of be-coming. This normative view would make us
> understand that life is not what it *is* but a project that could be perfected and
> *ought to be* realized. (Jafari 1386, 215)

Since the inception of the Enlightenment Tradition, which resulted in the
shunning of metaphysics in the context of what came to be known as *positive
sciences*, disciplinary thinkers tended to establish domains of research where
the empirical, rational, and intellectual dimensions are, first, separated, and,
then, set in contrast to each other. This finally led to two broad positions
within sciences (Empiricism versus Rationalism) at the expense of intellection within humanities. But Allama Jafari believes that the background
assumptions of humanities are of an intelligible nature, which can be solely
conceived through metaphysical analysis. In other words,

> within the natural sciences we may be able to employ synthetic and analytic
> approaches in studying material phenomena which are quantifiable, but within
> the humanities when we move further towards the "inner domains of the self"
> and the "scope of action," which is deeply interrelated with the "self" as an or-
> ganizing principle, we shall realize that by analyzing each phenomenon in this
> broad context we come willy-nilly in contact with metaphysical problematiques
> that are not quantifiable and also inaccessible to empirical methodologies (Jafari
> 1386, 217).

## LIFE-WORLD AND INSTRUMENTAL RATIONALITY

In analyzing modernity, disciplinary sociology has mainly focused on the onrush of formal rationality into the spheres of life that would be better off under the command of substantial rationality. Habermas is one of the acute sociologists who has elaborated upon the distinction that should be made between spheres of leben, where instrumental rationality should rule supreme and where substantive rationality should, so to speak, be the only game in town. But the crisis of modernity, which has led to the problem of *instrumentalization* of life, is not solely due to the demise of substantial rationality. The "absence of essential rationality" is the reason why the world of humanity is losing its vital quality. Allama Jafari believes that instrumentalization within humanities as a sociological problem is an expression of three deep-seated tendencies concomitant with modernism that is traceable to the philosophical currents of humanistic Europe. He discerns three trends as follows:

1. Hedonism: Within modernity the grand meta-narrative is of reduction of life that replaces the "intellectual" by the "empirical." This meta-turn has brought us to such a point that all attempts within human existence are reduced to be judged by the index of "pleasure." Without the presence of this principle, which is devoid of any intelligible interiority, life is deemed to be meaningless. In other words, the meaning of life has been geared to the notion of pleasure, and the notion of pleasure has been reduced to the level of sensation. Without realization of this sensual concept of pleasure, human existence is announced to be devoid of meaning. But, the question is, how has this happened? Of course, we admit that pleasure is of a vital significance in the constitution of the well-being of the human person, but this principle should be actualized in the course of self-realization, which is based on "Ultimate Reality," as without cordial relation with this "Telos" human beings cannot be realized in terms of "individuation." The sensualization of existence has occurred due to a mistaken conception of values and virtues and their respective locus within the overall context of metaphysical discernment. In other words, once you agree that values are contractual at all levels and in all aspects you will not leave any crucial room for covenantal interpretation of ethics.

2. Power: When we talk about human existence we need to make a distinction between two forms or levels of leben, i.e., "natural life" and "intelligible life," as this distinction or lack of it would surely define the contours and characters of our conceptions of society, social life, existence, individual and many other significant concepts related to human life. Having made this distinction, we would realize that there are two forms of power

conceptions within the intelligible life. Whenever we mention the concept of power we intend the ability to transform and be-coming, which should be always non-reducible and at the service of humanity, but what Hobbes, Nietzsche and their likes talk about is reduced notions of power, which are at the service of "natural life" and at the service of the ruling classes.
3. Utilitarianism: There is no doubt that each human person should take into consideration the "utility" of an action as the "moral worth" of an action should not be disconnected from its contribution to the overall utility, which is interrelated to happiness and pleasure. But, the question is not to deny the role of utility in the constitution of self and society. On the contrary, the problem has arisen from the point where seeking utility has become the sole purpose of life, and, as a matter of fact in, contradistinction to "right," "truth," and "real." (Jafari 1386, 215–16)

In other words, the question of the humanities and the predicament of human sciences, which are another way of problematizing the dilemmas of "modern man," are due to the fact that the locus of "Ultimate Reality" in the constitution of the self and society has disappeared, and the saga of this disappearance is in need of deconstruction.

## HUMAN SCIENCES AND METAPHYSICAL IMPERATIVES

Allama Jafari believes that the contemporary crises which have enveloped the life of humanity are closely related to the lack of metaphysical discernment and so-called scientific theories, which have emptied the humanity of human beings by reducing their being-ness to sub-human levels of "is-ness." He conceptualizes this reduction, which has created catastrophic consequences, not only within human sciences as fields of research but for humanity at large as well, in the form of five aspects: of "excessive naturalism," "evolution and transformism," "the will to power," "Freudianism," and "Malthusianism." In his view, each of these positions may have been qualified as scientific positions but by neglecting the pivotal locus of "human self as an individuated possibility" they have missed the crucial distinction by which a theory could be qualified as a vision of reality in the context of the human sciences.

### Excessive Naturalism

Jafari believes that, as he expresses it,

the contemporary excessive naturalism which we witness within the modernist paradigm is not the cause but the effect of an earlier dissipation towards Nature (and the knowledge of natural phenomena). If man could in his pursuits, in general, and in his intellectual pursuits, in particular, adopt a moderate attitude we would not witness either an excessive or dissipative approach towards the Natural Order, which led to darkness and has driven towards a kind of disease, which can only be conceptualized as "alienation." One wonders what damage the excessive or dissipative approach to Nature and the role of humanities in this drama have caused in the past. One also wonders at how the contemporary indulgence towards naturalistic interpretation has devastated the growth of knowledge. The dissipative inclination in matters of Nature in the past created a situation whereby contemporary thinkers could make us believe that in scientific activities either of "analytic" or "synthetic" kinds we are to deal with quantifiable matters. No doubt the quantification of knowledge is an irresistible ideal within the natural sciences, but the proponents of naturalism fail to note that within the humanities and social sciences as we move towards issues of identity, self, and the being of the human person the question becomes less quantifiable and more of a metaphysical nature. (Jafari 1386, 216–17)

## Evolution and Transformism

The hypothesis, or doctrine, that living beings have originated by the modification of some other previously existing forms of living matter is opposed to abiogenesis. Allama Jafari argues that reductionism could be traced to Lamarckian and Darwinian worldviews, which have been used to deny the sacrality of life. He further contends that

> although the theories of Darwin and Lamarck have been employed to disqualify the cordial relationship between Atman and Brahman as well as the divinity of human life, these discourses have come to a dead-end as the problem of "origin" is a matter of dispute and by no means an evident proof. In addition, observing the process of the embryonic emergence of the human organism cannot hinder the birth of magnanimity and dignity in the life of humanity. (Jafari 1386, 218)

## Will to Power

*Der Wille zur Macht* is a prominent concept in the philosophy of Friedrich Nietzsche and has been endorsed by many Machiavellians in contemporary politics. Allama Jafari argues that

> this seemingly scientific theory has deeply neglected an important dimension of human self, i.e., the power of self to control its activities in an integral fashion. This "power" is the most fundamental condition for the realization of "intelligible life" in relation to the human person both individually and collectively. The advocates of the Nietzschean thesis of *Der Wille zur Macht* are unable to answer the significant question within the field of ethics, namely: Is a powerful

person the one who forces others to live in accordance to his will or the one who concedes to the "right" of others without conditioning their lives based on his whims? It is self-evident that the true power is the ability to live in harmony with others, and that the weakest person is the one who is unable to concede to the rights of others. (Jafari 1386, 219)

Another important issue which Allama Jafari has reflected upon is the question of normativity within the social sciences and humanities, which has been conceptualized time and again as a descriptive problematique within the historiography of social sciences and cultural studies. In his words,

one needs to make a distinction between what the advocates of the "will to power" describe and prescribe as when they argue, for instance, that "the supermen have always been ruling the world." Is this a description or a prescription? The delicate line between these methodological approaches needs to be conceptualized carefully as each of them rests upon a different metaphysical worldview, and should not be treated as objective narration within the human sciences by disciplinary sociologists. (Jafari 1386, 219)

## Freudianism

Allama Jafari is of the opinion that Freud's theory, by focusing on "sexual instinct," is extreme because, as he puts it, it reduces

the complexity of human identity, which is incomprehensible without taking into consideration the normative infrastructures of the human soul. Of course, it is undeniable that certain aspects of Freudian theories on dreams, the unconscious, consciousness, and levels of consciousness are of importance, but it is also irrefutable that Freud's dismissive approach towards possibilities of self-realization, his conceptualization of religion, religiosity, and the ethicalness of the human self, and issues of this kind wrought great havoc on the human sciences, and, consequently, on human life as the central subject of the humanities. By demonstrating a methodological reluctance towards non-quantifiable aspects of human life, Freud practically disqualified himself as a competent theorist in the field of human existence, where issues of spirituality, values, virtues and existential ideals rule supreme. In other words, by denying the authenticity of "conscience" as a pivotal faculty in sustaining decency within the context of the life-world, Freud demonstrated that he had not moved beyond the frontiers of "natural life," and that he was also negligent about the possibility of "intelligible life" within the parameters of his naturalistic frame of reference. (Jafari 1386, 219)

## Malthusianism

Malthus argued that man, sooner or later, will run up against himself and that the population of mankind will eventually outstrip man's ability to supply himself with the necessities of life. Malthus' doctrine, as stated in his *Essay on the Principles of Population*, was based on the axiom that population increases in a geometric ratio while the means of subsistence increases in an arithmetic ratio. Allama Jafari argues that the Malthusian doctrine seems to suggest that we need to resort to war or any unethical means

> in order to stave off the explosion of population. But these approaches are indecent and unethically inhumane. Besides, the Malthusian doctrine is not only unethically wrong but principally unfounded, and we can mention three of these principles which invalidate the reasonability of this doctrine. The primary problem with the Malthusian model is its negligence with regard to the field of technology which has enabled us to employ industrial models in increasing food production parallel to population increase. The second critique which could be leveled at the Malthusian doctrine is a detailed calculation of the cost which various states force upon their nations by making unnecessary weapons of mass destruction as well as employing unfair policies of distribution of wealth and resources which have led to the poverty of the majority of humanity. This is a clear negation of the Malthusian doctrine, which relates the lack of resources to the increasing of population rather than realizing the role of unjust policies. Thirdly, we can mention the ability of the humans in controlling the birthrate in a conscious fashion, which is prescribed by the religious canon in the Islamic Tradition. (Jafari 1386, 221)

The Malthusian doctrine, which has influenced the parameters of the human sciences by reducing the role of "human sensibility" in the constitution of the self and society, is based on the argument that there are two principal hungers that nature has instilled in man, that for food and that for sex. Malthus was of the view that neither of these hungers could ever be quelled or controlled. But for Jafari this myopic observation is a reflection of naturalistic philosophies, which reduce the pivotal role of "intelligible life" in the constitution of social life. He argues that

> those who endorse this trend are either ignorant or by purpose advocate reductionism in an ontological fashion, which narrows the scope of life into utilitarianism. This cripples humanities as branches of knowledge within our societies, and would lead to reification of man rather than the elevation of the human self by reducing the humanness of the human self through weapons of mass persuasion. (Jafari 1386, 222)

The impact of humanities has declined within the context of naturalistic-oriented societies of our global world, where technologism[1] seems to be the only game in the town. It is undeniable, nevertheless, Allama Jafari says, that humanism in its integral sense requires that

> the sacred dimension of human identity is not denied but appropriated, as its absence would lead to annihilation of humanity. [This] has been stressed by great

souls in the West as well as in the East, by thinkers such as Albert Schweitzer, Alexis Carrel, Alfred North Whitehead, and many great others. In other words, modernism has denied the "authentic essence of human self," which is the only "permanent anchorage" in the course of history, without which there will be no sign of humanity and, by extension, no trace of human sciences. . . . This essential substance is preservable provided we find answers for the following questions, i.e., 1) Who am I? 2) Whence have I come? 3) Whereto have I come? 4) Who am I with? 5) What for have I come? and 6) Whereto am I heading? (Jafari 1386, 222)

## NOTE

1. The concept of "Technologism" refers to the following aspects within the human sciences:

- Predictability: The conviction that technology and its outcome as well as effects are predictable. Hence, we can plan, design, or even engineer our lives and our future in technological ways.
- Calculability: The conviction that technology, with its procedures and outcomes, are all calculable, i.e., recordable, quantifiable, and computable. Hence, we can organize our lives and future in quantifiable and calculable terms.
- Manageability: Building on predictability and calculability, human beings come to believe that we can manipulate technology as well as our lives and future according to our desires.
- Controllability: Finally, with the help of all these capacities of technology, modern men/women come to believe that technology as well as human lives and the future under its command are all under control.

## Chapter Five

# Rationality, Leben, and Intelligible Life

Within sociology, social theory, and social philosophy, the dominant thesis is the theory of rationalization. It is not an exaggeration to argue that the birth of sociology in its disciplinary form is concomitant with the emergence of rationality as a modern concept that belongs exclusively to the domain of *Aufklärung*, which, in Kant's perception, has determined, at least in part, what we are, what we think, and what we do today. In other words, to discuss the question of rationality is not solely a debate about a concept but is also an engagement at a complex level, which is of *weltanschauung* in nature. To paraphrase Seyed Jalal Al-e-Ahmad,[1] the question of rationality is the story of separation, which has fashioned the destiny of modern mentalité as an "Estranged Dasein" that has been thrown into the abyss of life without any *telos* in sight. The saga of rationalization is best captured in Weberian sociology, where Weber focuses on this issue by dividing it into two domains: (a) formal rationality and (b) substantive rationality. By the ascendance of formal rationality over substantive rationality, the quality of life decreases to a point where instrumentalization turns into the only game in the town. Critics of modernity tend to view the instrumentalization of the life-world as a result of the ascendance of formal over substantive rationality without venturing on the complexities of "rationality," which seems to be the core of the problem rather than the ascendance of formal rationality over its counterpart.

It is undeniable that the central contribution of Weber's thinking is the recognition of the dialectical interplay between formal versus substantive rationality, consumption versus production, choice versus life chances, class similarities versus distinctions, and self-control versus conformity in shaping the contemporary modern world. But the critics of modernity, who view the entire modern episteme in a critical fashion, believe that the "rationalization of reason," "dissociation of reason from the intellect," and "disarticulation of the intellect from revelation" have had catastrophic consequences for the very contours as well as content of human life. What people like Weber looked at is a small aspect of a larger problem, where issues of formal versus substantive rationality occupy insignificant positions. Ritzer, for instance, made a contribution to sociological theory by extending Weber's thesis about rationality and rationalization. His is a critique of rationality, which is appropriate in so far as rationality emerges as a nightmare in contemporary social and political organizations. He argues for agency and creativity within the framework of freedom rather than something else that may cater for the "good life" from tradition. What primordial critics of modernity, such as Allama Jafari, have in mind is the whole question of what should form the fulfillment for the modern man. The issue is highly complex and even contentious, and confining the problem to the realms of formal rationality versus substantive rationality will not solve the predicament of humanity, as the disciplinary approach is unable to venture beyond the critique of rationality by exploring the problem of human destiny any further.[2] This leads us to Allama Jafari's central debate, which is best known as "intelligible life", namely a critical thesis of contemporary sociological theories on self and society or self-actualization and progress, both horizontally and vertically. Allama has never been debated within sociological discourses as a social theorist, and there is almost no trace of his central thesis, which is of theoretical significance within the philosophical/sociological/theoretical debates on "life-world," "life-style," "world-system," "realm of necessity," and "realm of freedom." This debate is a humble attempt to revitalize interest in Allama Jafari's social thought in an intercivilizational fashion, which is little heard of within the global community of social scientists.

## ANTHROPOLOGY REVISITED

When speaking of anthropology, we need to be conscious of different connotations in relation to this concept, depending on paradigms, contexts, and intellectual systems, since what is meant by this term within disciplinary discourses surely differs from primordial approaches to the same concept. The term "anthropology" was used for first time in English in 1593 in referring to the study of human beings universally, i.e., everywhere and throughout time. It is argued that disciplinary anthropology has its intellectual origins in both the "natural sciences" and the "humanities." Marvin Harris, the contemporary historian of anthropology, indicates two major frameworks within which disciplinary anthropology has arisen: interest in comparisons of people over space, and interest in long-term human processes or humans as viewed through time.

Most scholars consider modern anthropology as an outgrowth of the Age of Enlightenment, a period when Europeans attempted to systematically study human behavior, the known varieties of which had been increasing since the 15th century as a result of the first European colonization wave. The traditions of jurisprudence, history, philology, and sociology then evolved into something more closely resembling the modern views of these disciplines and informed the development of the social sciences, of which anthropology was a part. Developments in the systematic study of ancient civilizations through the disciplines of Classics and Egyptology informed archaeology and, eventually, social anthropology, as did the study of East and South Asian languages and cultures. At the same time, the Romantic reaction to the Enlightenment produced thinkers, such as Johann Gottfried Herder and later Wilhelm Dilthey, whose work formed the basis for the "concept of "culture," which is central to the discipline. Institutionally, anthropology emerged from the development of natural history that occurred during the European colonization of the 17th, 18th, 19th, and 20th centuries. Programs of ethnographic study originated in this era as the study of the "primitive" humans overseen by colonial administrations.

There was a tendency in late 18th-century Enlightenment thought to understand human society as natural phenomena that behaved in accordance with certain principles and that could be observed empirically. In some ways, studying the language, culture, physiology, and artifacts of European colonies was not unlike studying the flora and fauna of those places. Early anthropology was divided between proponents of unilinealism, who argued that all societies passed through a single evolutionary process, from the most "primitive" to the most "advanced," and various forms of non-lineal theorists, who tended to subscribe to ideas such as diffusionism. Most 19th-century social theorists, including anthropologists, viewed non-European societies as windows onto the pre-industrial human past. As academic disciplines began to differentiate over the course of the 19th century, anthropology grew increasingly distinct from the biological approach of natural history, on the one hand, and purely historical or literary fields, such as Classics, on the other. A common criticism has been that many social science scholars (such as economists, sociologists, and psychologists) in Western countries focus disproportionately on Western subjects, while anthropology focuses disproportionately on the "Other"; this has changed over the last part of the 20th century, as anthropologists increasingly also study Western subjects, particularly variation across class, region, or ethnicity within Western societies, and other social scientists increasingly take a global view of their fields.

In the 20th century, academic disciplines have often been institutionally divided into three broad domains. The natural and biological *sciences* seek to derive general laws through reproducible and verifiable experiments. The *humanities* generally study local traditions, through their history, literature, music, and arts, with an emphasis on understanding particular individuals, events, or eras. The *social sciences* have generally attempted to develop scientific methods to understand social phenomena in a generalizable way, though usually with methods distinct from those of the natural sciences. In particular, social sciences often develop statistical descriptions rather than general laws as derived in physics or chemistry, or they may explain individual cases through more general principles, as in many fields of psychology. Anthropology does not easily fit into one of these categories, and different branches of anthropology draw on one or more of these domains. Anthropology, as it emerged among the colonial powers, has generally taken a different path than that in the countries of southern and central Europe (Italy, Greece, and successors to the Austro-Hungarian and Ottoman empires). In the former, the encounter with multiple, distinct cultures, often very different in organization and language from those of Europe, led to a continuing emphasis on cross-cultural comparison and receptiveness to certain kinds of cultural relativism. In the successor states of continental Europe, on the other hand, anthropologists often joined with folklorists and linguists in the nationalist/nation-building enterprise. Ethnologists in these countries tended to focus on differentiating among local ethnolinguistic groups, documenting local folk culture, and representing the prehistory of the "nation" through museums and other forms of public education. In this scheme, Russia occupied a middle position. On the one hand, it had a large Asian region of highly distinct, pre-industrial, often non-literate peoples, similar to the situation in the Americas; on the other hand, Russia also participated to some degree in the nationalist discourses of Central and Eastern Europe. After the Revolution of 1917, anthropology in the USSR and later the Soviet Bloc countries was highly shaped by the need to conform to Marxist theories of social evolution. (Wallerstein 2003, 453-66)

In other words, the term "anthropology" seems to have a ring of technicality around its academic neck, which differs sharply from the fashion by which the same term is used in Persian by Allama Jafari, as he seems to read other interpretations of the concepts of "human" and "discourse." The term used by Allama Jafari in Persian is *Ensan-Shenasi*. The first part is equivalent to the English term "human," and the second part refers to the epistemological dimension embedded in the terms "discourse" and "logy" in English. In the disciplinary discourses on anthropology, we are working with terms such as "evolution," "natural course of history," and "biological models," which together build up a naturalistic paradigm in conceptualizing the complex historical traits of the *homo sapiens*. Although the disciplinary anthropologists do not customarily step beyond this empirical level of theorizing, it is doubtless that the overarching unit-idea that holds this diverse form of analyses is the notion of "struggle for existence" or "the survival of the fittest."

Of course, ultra-empirical generalizations are not approved of by disciplinary anthropologists, based on the arguments that these generalizations lack two fundamental criteria of anthropology, i.e., proper empirical comparisons and empirical fieldworks. Instead, modern anthropologists consider a discourse as modern within anthropological domains wherever the anthropologist leaves his/her hometown by studying other cultures besides his/her own. But even these qualifications have not led disciplinary anthropology and modern anthropologists to move beyond the above-mentioned unit-ideas of "struggle" and "survival."

In Allama Jafari's view, briefly speaking, this corresponds to the primary level of his conceptual model, where "naturalism" rules supreme, and for which he coins the phrase "natural life." But this is not the only level on which human beings can and should operate, as the "self" is capable of overcoming conflicts, wars, atrocities, genocides, and clashes; instead they should work on "solidarity," "cooperation," and "charity" at an intensively durable level. We need to look at his definitions on "natural life," "intelligible life," and "anthropology," as these issues make up the theoretical body of his social thought, which may prove to be constructive sociologically as well as within the broader contexts of social theory and social philosophy.

## NATURAL LIFE

Allama Jafari divides life into two domains of "natural life" and "intelligible life." He argues that

> the decisive factors that cause this distinction consist of internal factors, such as human instincts that cannot be managed except through the power of human character, which is backed up by reason and conscience, for otherwise the instinctual makeup of the human being does not know any limit and looks incessantly for more sensual satisfaction. They also include external factors that are related to social relations, which reflect the necessity of social life, and these are mostly self-referential in character. (Jafari 1387, 20–21)

These two sets of factors have created in the course of history two forms of life-world, which, in the Jafarian scheme of things, is divided into the two following realms:

1. The first realm is related to people who have chosen to ignore the imperatives of "conscience" in the constitution of their lives and, instead, apply

the rules of instinctual inclinations in their existence. Besides, it should be added that this group has been inclined to conform to "social frames", no matter what their relevance in the constitution of "human eschatology".
2. The second realm belongs to people who have taken the imperatives of "conscience" and "reason" seriously by actualizing their imperatives in the context of selfhood. (Jafari 1387, 21)

In other words, Allama Jafari argues that the distinction of life-worlds based on these sets of forms, styles and make-ups rests on the kind of definition we have about human beings. To put it differently, our anthropology influences the character of our worldview and vice versa. Based on these axioms, one could argue that the proponents of the "natural life" view the scope of life in a very factual fashion by building solely on, as Allama Jafari puts it, "the nature of human self as it 'is' without realizing the ideal dimension of the human being, which is based on the nature of the human self as it 'ought to be'" (Jafari 1387, 22).

Based on this ontological distinction, which has methodological consequences in the context of social theory and sociological theory, Allama Jafari renounces the sociologism of Durkheim and the Durkheimians by arguing that

> the excessive inclinations towards "sociologism" have created insurmountable dilemmas in relation to the individual and society. Durkheim's ontological commitment deprives humanity of the possibility of moving from a life under the parameters of "natural life" to an "intelligible life order," which is prominently illustrated by the notion of "autonomy" as a unique human possibility. (Jafari 1387, 22–33)

Elsewhere, Allama Jafari argues that "the most salient dimension of life, which distinguishes the realms of animate from the inanimate, is the question of 'autonomy' within the human existential order" (Jafari 1387, 33). In other words, the rule of naturalism has driven humanity towards a colossal shift from "divinization" towards "reification." Jafari is of the view that this current cannot be overcome "without the presence of a firm character, which could manage the immense affairs of the self in relation to the complexities of leben" (33).

To put it otherwise, the fragmentalization of the self in the context of modernity is admitted by Allama Jafari as a sociological fact, but he does not consider this a "natural" consequence of human social history. On the contrary, he views this as a pathology and a direct consequence of, as he puts it, "a compartmentalization of science, which, in turn, is a sign of a deeper crisis, i.e., the fragmentalization of the self. In healing this pathological disease, we need to have an integral approach which is capable of considering the self in its totality" (Jafari 1387, 32).

According to Allama Jafari, the dominance of the "natural life-paradigm" is not a very *natural* phenomenon, as many naturalist thinkers may like to suggest, as this relates to inability of disciplinary thinkers in building "coherent *weltbild* as well as their inability in realizing their own latent background assumptions, which operate as tacit worldview, even in the context of the so-called empirical sciences" (Jafari 1387, 34).

## INTELLIGIBLE LIFE

It may be of interest to know that Allama Jafari did not propose the debate on "intelligible life" as a solely theoretical issue, which could be discussed by academics without having any practical consequences. On the contrary, without realizing the boundaries of human possibility in relation to the material and the spiritual dimensions nobody can fathom the contours of life either in an individual or collective form. Consequently, humanity would fail to embark upon the path of growth and self-realization. In other words, Jafari argues that the realization of "intelligible life" is not a utopian ideal, but a human-historical necessity, whose imperativeness has not only been realized by Eastern intellectuals but also by prominent Occidental philosophers, such as Alfred North Whitehead who believed that "We stand at a moment when the course of history depends upon the calm reasonableness arising from a religious public opinion" (cited by Jafari, 1387, 54).

In other words, the sociological necessity of realizing the distinction between "natural life" and "intelligible life" is beyond sensible doubt, and a reasonable assessment of social life would surely reveal the possibility of self-transcendence as well as the viciousness of denying the possibility of man going beyond the boundaries of "naturalistic" interpretations of leben.

Allama Jafari proposes an anthropological principle, which is employed within his theoretical paradigm through and through in relation to various dimensions of social and individual life. This significant principle, he explains, "which is of great importance within the anthropological domain, is the vital connection between two realms of 'is' and 'ought to' that has been sorely neglected within the context of disciplinary social sciences" (Jafari 1387, 55). Jafari is of the opinion that "without realizing the delicate inter-relationship between these two realms surely our ontology and anthropology would encounter grave obstacles, and these would aggravate the intensity of our predicament" (55).

## INTELLIGIBLE LIFE DEFINED

Allama Jafari has a particular approach to the question of "intelligibility," which could be compared to disciplinary concepts such as "rationality," "reasonability," and "formal/substantive rationality." The concept of "intelligibility" may seem similar to disciplinary discourses of Weberian or Habermasian social theory, but there are fundamental differences between them, as Allama Jafari argues that

> the actualization of "intelligible life" in the contexts of self and society is based upon interaction between permanent and contingent dimensions. Although the contours of the human self are changeable, the dominant features of his/her being enjoy a form of unicity that is, in turn, dependent upon "intelligible principles" and "rational laws." (Jafari 1387, 58)

The constant use of the concepts such as "rational," "intelligible," or "reasonability" by Allama Jafari compels us to reflect on the definitions that he attaches to these concepts, as they may differ from what we customarily encounter in disciplinary discourses. He defines intelligible life as

> a conscious life, which is based upon a distinguished awareness about the realms of "necessity" and the domains of "freedom," as well as a conscious attempt in overcoming the seemingly deterministic dimensions of life by exercising freedom in the course of evolutionary progress as this would enhance the power of the human self by assisting us to realize the grand goal of life, which is participation in the cosmic movement towards blissful perfection. (Jafari 1387, 59)

This is what Jafari means by "intelligible life," i.e., a life that distinguishes between two grand domains of "necessity" and "freedom," as well as the decisive role played by consciousness in actualizing the latent human possibilities with reference to cosmic reality, which is not of a contractual nature but, rather, of covenantal design. However, one may wonder what he means by "rationality" in the context of "intelligible life."

### The Idea of Reasonability in "Intelligible Life"

We need to deconstruct the Jafarian discourse on reason, as Jafari has in mind three different, but interrelated, discourses on the issue, which may look as disparate matters and irrelevant to questions of rationality, rationalization, reason, reasonability, and intelligibility by social theorists. First, we have the discourse on "rationalism" within the Occidental context; then second, the discourse on the "minimalist notion of reason," and third, debates on the "maximalist notion of reason," which have been discussed by both Oriental and Occidental thinkers. Some may think that Allama Jafari is referring to reasonability or intelligibility in the minimalist tradition, which has been extensively shunned by wisdom-philosophers and Gnostics in both the West and the East. There is a possibility, he says, that

> critics may assume that the notion of "intelligible life" is related to the position taken by rationalists versus empiricists, and that the concept of intelligibility is extracted from this philosophical position within the Occidental history of ideas. . . . Besides, we should remember that wisdom-philosophers, Gnostics and philosophers of both the East and the West have divided Reason into three different kinds: a) theoretical reason, b) practical reason, and c) holistic reason. There should not be any doubt that by "reasonable" or "intelligible" in the context of "intelligible life" we do not mean the "minimalist" notion of theoretical reason. While there is no dispute that it is of great instrumental significance in realizing aspects of human existence, at the same time it is doubtless that the scope of instrumental rationality should be delimited as, to use a metaphor, it is futile to expect "hearing" from eye-sight, or vice versa. Thus, it should be realized that within the paradigm of "intelligible life," we do not deny the realm of "is-ness" and "necessity," which is, or could be, of use in the constitution of self and society. However, in accordance with the "intelligible paradigm," we make a bridge between the domain of "is-ness" and "ought to." (Jafari 1387, 57–68)

Allama Jafari further explains:

> Within the "intelligible paradigm," theoretical reason, on one side, and practical reason (which is another term for the conscious, active and mobilizing conscience), on the other side, are at the disposal of the growing and perfection-seeking personality. To put it differently, we should be certain that the "intelligible" within the "intelligible paradigm" has nothing to do with "rationalism," and is surely different from formal rationality, as the scope of intelligibility envelopes the entire gamut of human existence in all domains, material as well as spiritual. It should not be treated in terms of formal rationality and substantive rationality, which are directed at the serial dimensions of life solely in the context of contractual social life. (Jafari 1387, 67–75)

## FUNDAMENTALS OF INTELLIGIBLE LIFE

The question of the "intelligible life-paradigm" needs to be deconstructed in the sociological sense, as the significance of this model has not been yet realized in metasociological parlance. Allama Jafari seems to suggest that

> humanity has been extensively under the spell of "egocentric nature," which has caused damage in terms of "realization of wonderful possibilities" by driving

human society as well as social relations in a given community towards alienation, fragmentation, and reification. (Jafari 1387, 74)

In other words, he believes that the transformation of life, in its individual as
well as collective sense, needs to be based on certain fundamentals, and he
has categorized them in the following fashion:

## Conscious Life

Allama Jafari divides the project of leben into two broad camps of "consciousness" and "unconsciousness." He holds that there is a significant distinction between these two modes of being in life as, as he puts it,

> in a life based on the "unconscious mode," the self lacks an integral vision of real-
> ity. This leads to an inherent disability in distinguishing between "I" from "He,"
> and "I" from "It." On the other hand, a life based on "conscious modality" is a life
> where the human self follows certain principles and values which are instrumental
> in actualizing the latent potentialities of being, which leads to an individuation
> of higher degree. This could not occur unless the human self is aware of the gal-
> vanizing potentialities of leben. This realization is intertwined with "existential
> awareness." In other words, the "intelligible life" is another term for the "religious
> life," which, in turn, is synonymous with "consciousness" and "awareness." To
> put it differently, self-consciousness is the result of intellectual and existential
> endeavors, which are based on a conscious realization of the realms of "is-ness"
> and the domains of "ought to," as well as efforts to overcome Hume's Guillotine
> problem, which exists between these two. (Jafari 1387, 78–80)

## Freedom and Necessity

Within the context of humanities and social sciences, the question of freedom
and necessity has been extensively debated by sociologists and philosophers.
The crux of these discussions could be summarized as an attempt to *reconcile*
the *irreconcilable*. However, Allama Jafari believes that to leave the debate at
this stage is not only academically wrong but is also existentially harmful, as
this is a significant debate, whose importance goes beyond conceptuality. In
other words, the importance of this problematique is of vital consequence in
the constitution of self and society. As Allama Jafari explains, to understand
this issue

> is of great importance for those interested in realization of intelligibility in an
> integral fashion, both individually and collectively. In other words, to know the
> scope of freedom and conceive the gamut of necessity are of such vital impor-
> tance that it would not be an exaggeration to contend that life without realizing

the frontiers of these two domains could not be considered as human leben. Of great significance in this debate is the distinction which should be made between three different, but interrelated, stages of freedom, i.e., a) releasement, b) liberty, and c) authority.[3] Those who view life either in terms of determinism or indeterminism have not realized the substantive distinctions which exist between these various modes of freedom, as at the first level man is under the tutelage of passions of various kinds without having the ability to discern the complexities of individuation, while at the second level self is released from bondages and conditions, in addition to the ability of choosing a path among many possibilities. But, this liberty is not yet of qualitative nature. This is to argue that the self at the level of liberty is still unable to discern between virtues and vices and embark upon the virtuous path. This is a grave misunderstanding in the context of social theory, which has had sociopolitical as well as existential consequences for the self and society as we have mistaken liberty with autonomy. In other words, in the state of "autonomy" the human self has achieved an authority to manage and supervise the immense vitality of life, based on distinguishing between positive and negative poles, and employing the possibility of liberty in achieving a virtuous life. The distinction between the three levels of freedom is not only of metaphysical importance but also has longstanding consequences for the self in all its four dimensional figurations. (Jafari 1387, 80–84)

In other words, Allama Jafari views the significance of freedom in its threefold fashion in relation to "intelligible life" in a sociological manner. As he puts it:

The level of progress in human society is interrelated with the question of autonomy. This is to say, progress or growth is proportional to the degree of actualization of liberty in an autonomous fashion as this reflects the realization of the "intelligible paradigm" in the constitution of the self and society. (Jafari 1387, 84)

## Human Growth and Ideals

The role that ideals play in human societies is one of the most complex issues in the human sciences. It would not be farfetched to argue that the history of political ideas has been shaped through the dialectics of ideas and ideals within the context of the self and society. But these ideals are not all of the same character, and human societies have been exposed to different sets of ideals in the course of history, which has been greatly restricted by ruling elites, who have imposed their will in the minds and hearts of human civilizations since time immemorial. In Jafari's words:

The history of humanity is not the integral story of realization of lofty ideals and an example of actualization of the innate possibilities of primordial nature, because the ruling class has always inhibited the free flow of the wonderful possibilities of authentic desires of human beings by either repressing them or managing them along prescribed lines, which have been dictated by power. To put it in other words, we are able to discern an actual state of affairs in diverse human societies where institutions are invented that are meant to express the totality of human civilizations and the civil ethos of humanity, but a critical assessment would readily reveal that this is not the case. We can discern that human possibility is more than what historical social institutions in their totality have been able to actualize. This leads us to the fact that no society has been able to actualize the wonderful possibilities of what primordial nature is capable of. There are exceptions to this rule, and that is those of minorities who have been able to display the full possibility of being an integral human self. One of the most authentic dimensions of human nature, which has been incessantly displayed during the long history of mankind, is the ability to live a good life and the capability to actualize all the virtuous potentials which could be instrumental in achieving the felicitous life. This dimension of the human self is undeniable except by sophistry and fallacious arguments. Thus, the question is, what kind of life-paradigm is compatible with this authentic dimension of the human self? (Jafari 1387, 87–88)

Allama Jafari answers this question in a straightforward fashion by stating that

A truthfully felicitous life is not conceivable except within the parameters of "intelligible life." This is to argue that the human personality is in dire need of "intelligibility" in the course of its realization as without it life would lose the possibility of renewality, which is the sole property of "intelligibility." Of course, by renewality and "forward march" we do not mean material renewalness or progress in serial fashion and within time and space. On the contrary, the point is the ability to transform the rudimentary and unprocessed emotions into elevated sensibilities and the partial picturing of life into a holistic vision of reality in an integral fashion. These two transformative moves would pave the way for the third decisive change, namely: the chance to enhance the emergence of a kind of will that is married with "liberty" and is conscious of the possibility of human autonomy or the self's capability to choose the virtuous path. (Jafari 1387, 88–89)

In other words, the ideal of "'intelligibility' refers to first principles which simultaneously safeguard the possibility of self-renewality and the unity of self in the midst of diversities" (Jafari, 1387, 92).

### Realization and the Ultimate Telos of Life

By distinguishing between two paradigms of Naturalism and Transcendentalism, Allama Jafari seems to be suggesting that as long as individuals are under the spell of the "natural self," which feels joy in being in the state of "liberty," there would be no possibility to raise the question of the "Ultimate Telos of Life." Additionally, for people who view life through the prism of naturalism, the reality of such a realization that aims at ultimate reality is incomprehensible as comprehension of this magnificent reality is conditioned by realization of two necessary premises, as without them any debate on "telos," "reality," "ultimate reality," and "the life based on lofty ideals" would sound nonsensical. (Jafari 1387, 92–93)

The two inalienable premises that should be taken into consideration consist of

1. Adequate use of "reason" in a proportional fashion in collaboration with "conscience," in conjunction with "intuitive primordial perceptions."
2. Serious will in connecting praxis and theory at the disposal of telos of life in terms of Ultimate Reality, i.e., the ability to distinguish between the "Metaphorical I" and the "Real I," as the unity of self is not conceivable as long as human existence is under the spell of metaphoricality. (Jafari 1387, 92–95)

## The Path of Intelligible Evolution

One of the significant questions that occupies the project of Jafarian social theory is the possibility of assessing the intellectual growth of the human individual without referring to exterior indices, such as urbanization, industrialization, advancement of technology and IT, and so on. With regard to the issue of the parameters of intelligible evolution, Allama Jafari notes:

This question is of profound importance in conceptualizing the paradigm of "intelligible life," as inability to fathom the longstanding consequences of the distinction between "public growth" and "individuated growth" has led to a miscalculation by believing that the progress, for instance, of the twentieth century means, automatically, the actualization of all these modern ideals in the soul of each person who happens by accident live in this century. We need to realize that the intelligible paradigm in the course of evolution of intellectual goals consists of two prominent dimensions, i.e., a) the teleological dimension and b) the instrumental dimension. (Jafari 1387, 96–97)

In brief, Allama Jafari believes that "intellectual growth" is possible and that this possibility is conceivable provided we are able to realize the grandiose potentiality of the spirit as a fundamental truth in the constitution of the human self. In other words, the elevation and ascension of the self in either individual or social dimensions are impossible to fathom as long as we are, as Allama writes, "operating under the narrow and darkening parameters of the natural life-paradigm" (Jafari 1387, 98).

## DIMENSIONS OF INTELLIGIBLE LIFE

One of the heated debates within modernity is the question of liberty. The institutionalization of freedom has been the yardstick of social progress and individual emancipation by philosophers, social theorists, and sociologists within the paradigm of the Enlightenment Tradition. *Aufklärungists* tend to accuse their opponents by resorting to the concept of "freedom," as in their view those without the paradigm of *Aufklärung* are on the wrong side of history. Based on this disciplinary generalization, thinkers such as Allama Jafari would willy-nilly fall outside the parameters of enlightenment in the generic sense of the term and not only in the technical sense with which this concept has come to be associated.

In other words, within this historiographical reading, Allama Jafari could be portrayed as an intellectual without any substantive commitment to the idea of freedom, which is supposedly the most wonderful dimension of human reality. But the question which should be asked is whether this characterization of the Jafarian project, or even that of any other *Unaufklärungist* social thinker, is justified or totally misplaced. The concise answer is that the project of Jafari is surely opposed to the disciplinary approach to the problematique of "freedom," but this is not equivalent to being against the discourse of freedom as a human possibility, which needs to be actualized both individually and socially. To put it differently, Jafari believes that it is possible for the human being to become a vital personality if freedom has been actualized in the soul of man as an act of "benevolent choice," which is not only semantically different from freedom but essentially distinguished from disciplinary conceptualizations of liberty *a la* Hobbes, Mill, Hume, Berlin, and Miguel Abensour, as freedom in the Jafarian sense is the ability to choose virtuously in the presence of vices.

To put it otherwise,

> if we do not choose virtuously in the presence of vices, we, *qua* human beings, have neither realized freedom as a faculty nor moved beyond the parameters of naturalistic history. This is to argue that we need to distinguish between evolutionary growth in the context of the naturalistic paradigm and the humane paradigm that is a reflection of intelligibility. (Jafari 1387, 106)

This distinction may lead us to the heart of modernism in its ontological dimension, which is intertwined with the question of "Nihilism," which shall emerge in the absence of the "synoptic teleology of leben" (Jafari 1387, 112).

We now turn to the dimensions of intelligible life, which are of significance in the domains of the self and society in the Jafarian perspective.

## Human Personality

Until recently, an author was an unproblematic concept; an author was someone who wrote a book. Roland Barthes' landmark essay, *The Death of Author*, however, seems to suggest that an author is not simply a *person*, but also a socially and historically constituted subject. Following Marx's reverse Hegelianism, that it is history that makes man and not, as Hegel supposed, man that makes history, Barthes emphasizes that an author does not exist prior to, or outside of, language. In other words, it is writing that makes an author, and not vice versa. Thus, the author cannot claim any absolute authority over his or her text, because, in some ways, he or she *did not write it*. This is not to say that someone named Saadi did not spend many years toiling away at a book called *Golestan*. Rather, we must re-think what it means when we associate Saadi and *Golestan*. Barthes throws the emphasis away from an all-knowing, unified, intending subject, as the site of production, onto language and, in so doing, hopes to liberate writing from the despotism of what he calls "the work," or what we have called *The Book*.

In other words, Barthes throws out what Allama Jafari seems to keep, i.e., the unified, intending subject that could supervise the project of life in a meaningful and autonomous fashion in the threefold domains of self, society, and cosmos. Of course, it is clear that the question is of a controversial nature, and we should not expect any straightforward answer to this issue as this debate is latently interrelated with the question of worldview and background assumptions, which play a vital role in the constitution of the "intelligible life-paradigm."

The role that the human personality may play in the constitution of the "intelligible life-paradigm" is one of the controversial themes that has been greatly debated by Allama Jafari who, unlike disciplinary thinkers, seems to disagree with "death of authors" discourses or "un-authorized discourses on the self," which are rampant in academia presently and play a decisive role in postmodernist discourses and cultures of human sciences.

Allama Jafari, on the contrary, suggests that

> Man has a nature which is of ascending character potentially. This sacrosanct nature is of universal character. Moreover, humanity as a species can enjoy a sense of "ethical unity" as mankind does share a common ethos, which is not of contingent nature but has its origin within the depths of the human soul. (Jafari 1387, 113–14)

## Morality and Ethics

Within contemporary discourses on religion, science, ethics and morality, we are often confronted with the two broad positions of "Relativism" and

"Rationalism," which seem to be irreconcilable and problematic whenever we attempt to fathom fundamental questions of "knowledge," "faith," and "veracity/falsehood." These issues within the sociology of knowledge have been problematized by sociologists such as Barry Barnes and David Bloor, who argue that empirical evidence suggests that knowledge is relative (Barnes and Bloor, 1982). Of course, this *a priori* argument leaves a fundamental question unanswered, i.e., how could empirical evidence suggest that knowledge is relative?

The Rationalists object that the Relativist perspective leads to undermining its own position by using terms like "true" or "false." On the other hand, the Relativists respond that they, like anyone else, judge propositions as "true" or "false" insofar as they meet, or fail to meet, locally acceptable standards of "truth" and "falsehood." The Relativists accept that their "preferences" and "evaluations" as to the truth-value of a proposition are context-relative (Barnes and Bloor, 1982). However Allama Jafari seems to embark upon a different path, not only in terms of ethics and morality or science and religion but also in the very manner we conceptualize these questions and any vital question that may be of decisive importance in the eschatology of the self and the constitution of society. In his seminal book *Intelligible Life,* he looks at the question of ethics in the context of "intelligible life" by arguing that

> it is needless to state that questions of ethics and morality and what is to be con-
> sidered as the ideal ethos have been greatly debated by prominent writers and
> philosophers since time immemorial. Of course, nobody would deny the signifi-
> cance of these debates with regard to the conduct of individuals, both psycho-
> logically and sociologically, as they have affected the very configurations of hu-
> man relationships across various cultures and societies. But, the most important
> question which is of decisive significance, and which, unfortunately, has been
> neglected by professional moral philosophers is the distinction which should be
> made between ethics in the context of "natural life" and morality in the context
> of "intelligible life." Disregarding this fundamental distinction would lead to
> futility by conceptualizing morality, ethicality and ethics in an absolute fashion,
> which is conceivably impossible without taking into consideration the supreme
> distinction between the two domains of existence. (Jafari 1387, 115–16)

Jafari's approach to the question of relativism has changed the very notion of relativism and its relevance for debates on morality, ethics, knowledge, science, and religion. In his view, we need to distinguish between the "context of discovery" and the "context of justification". However, these terms should not be understood in the Popperian fashion as Jafari works on a verti-cal ontology of the self and does not share the linear epistemology of modernism, which can be detected in Popperian moral philosophy.

In Kantian moral philosophy, we need to distinguish between "morality" and "legality." According to it, the legitimacy of power rests upon legality, which could arbiter between conflicting moral questions. Of course, the question of Marxian critiques in relation to the superstructure, which envelopes the legal domain as well, needs to be conceptualized, too, but we leave it aside as the main question here is the Jafarian approach to the question of morality in the context of intelligibility.

In other words, the distinction to which Kantians refer, and that has been conceptualized within modern legislative systems, seems to refer to the "natural life-paradigm," which has been disputed by Allama Jafari who argues that

> ethics within the paradigm of "intelligible life" cannot be at the disposal of the naturalistic legal system in an instrumental fashion, as the question of ethicality within an intelligible context is related to the "final cause" under the supervision of the "emancipated conscience." (Jafari 1387, 119)

In sum, Allama Jafari contends that morality within the parameters of intelligibility is incompatible,

> with sociologism, and cannot emerge within a contractual frame of reference, as "intelligible ethics" is based on being conscious about the interrelationship between the human being as "part" of the "whole" [which is of dialogical significance in the constitution of self and society]. (Jafari 1387, 119)

## Rights and Laws

The questions of "right" and "duty" are of vital importance within political philosophy and the sociology of law. This significance has not evaded the acute eye of Allama Jafari. He does not deny the relevance of "law" in the constitution of self and society in the disciplinary sense of the concept, which is conceptualized in sociological theories and moral philosophy discourses of modernity. On the contrary, he concedes that we need to have a sociology of body, but this sociology, which is based on a "social contract," has a specific task to solve, and this should not be wrongly interpreted as the end of "order," which is one of the byproducts of organizing human affairs.

In other words, Allama Jafari makes a distinction between the two domains of law by arguing that we have two levels of application, which could be termed as "contractual" and "covenantal." In the contractual domain, the law is devised to control what Hobbes terms as *bellum omnium contra omnes*, while the covenantal domain aims at organizing the spiritual affairs of human beings, since without this transcendental dimension, what is understood as "humanity" would not survive as an evolutionary species with the capacity to obtain growth, intelligibility, perfection, maturity, and high moral prominence. To put it differently,

> the intelligible life-paradigm is not meant to deny the significance of social institutions and legal systems, which are of sociological importance in terms of the social organization of human affairs. On the contrary, the question is of another order, i.e., for the growth of humanity we should not confine the frontiers of maturity to material interpretations of growth and actualization as the human being *qua* human person is capable of growing beyond the Hobbesian vision of self and society provided he is exposed to "spiritual excellence" and "conscientious prominence." This may cause mayhem in the camp of thinkers who stand for complete distinction between morality and legality by arguing that the question of right in legal terms cannot be interconnected with the concept of right in a moral sense. But, this distinction is not of objective order as many disciplinary thinkers seem to suggest. On the contrary, it relies on a specific reading of human anthropology, which disregards the ontological interrelationships between the realms of "is-ness" and the domains of "ought-to." In other words, within the intelligible paradigm, we argue that natural contracts are necessary but they are not sufficient for the becoming of the human self as an ascending being, which is in dire need of covenantal principles for self-realization and anti-alienation. (Jafari 1387, 120–24)

## Social Relations

Within modernist paradigms, we are faced with the two metatheoretical positions of "Utilitarianism" and "Leviathanism" in relation to *societas*, which seem to be based on a crude reductionism that, in Allama Jafari's words,

> aims to reduce the complexity of leben into a linear definition based on naturalism devoid of any transcendence and that views life in a myopic fashion by reference to "utility" and "aggression." Of course, there is no doubt that human life within the parameters of naturalism does indeed follow the prescribed lines of the Hobbesian ontology of power, but it would be a grave mistake to confine the scope of life within the borders of a naturalistic paradigm as leben has the capacity to be elevated onto higher levels of beingness. This is what we have termed as "intelligible life." In other words, the relation between human beings does not need to be solely based on utility or aggression as there is a higher logic, which follows a more benevolent reality and that is "humanistic foundation." To be certain, this foundation is not of pure idealistic nature, although it is a gracious ideal, but it should not be considered as idealistic in the sense that it is not realizable or is out of reach as this notion has come to be understood in [common English] today. (Jafari 1387, 124–26)

Allama Jafari further elaborates:

The very proposal that human societies cannot be established except by resorting to utility without any intelligible consideration is a delusive idea. This self-delusional approach to the question of "Ultimate Reality" would surely lead to a genocidal conclusion for humanity at large. To put it otherwise, societas and human relations need to be seen in the light of the intelligible paradigm, which aims to elevate the core of socialization based on "intelligible relationships." (Jafari 1387, 126)

## Science and Knowledge

Within the parameters of intelligible life the most fundamental dimension is "consciousness." But what is consciousness in contemporary discourses within the humanities and social sciences?

"Consciousness" is often used colloquially to describe a state of being awake and aware—responsive to the environment, in contrast to being asleep or in a coma. In philosophical and scientific discussions, however, the term is restricted to the specific state in which humans are mentally aware in such a way that they distinguish clearly between themselves (the thing being aware) and all other things and events. This "self-awareness" may involve thoughts, sensations, perceptions, moods, emotions, and dreams. (Flanagan 1995, 152)

The *Stanford Encyclopedia of Philosophy* states, for instance, that

Perhaps no aspect of mind is more familiar or more puzzling than consciousness and our conscious experience of self and world. The problem of consciousness is arguably the central issue in current theorizing about the mind. Despite the lack of any agreed upon theory of consciousness, there is a widespread, if less than universal, consensus that an adequate account of mind requires a clear understanding of it and its place in nature. We need to understand both what consciousness is and how it relates to other, non-conscious, aspects of reality. (Van Gulik 2004)

In other words,

A comprehensive understanding of consciousness will likely require theories of many types. One might usefully and without contradiction accept a diversity of models that each in their own way aim respectively to explain the physical, neural, cognitive, functional, representational and higher-order aspects of consciousness. There is unlikely to be any single theoretical perspective that suffices for explaining all the features of consciousness that we wish to understand. Thus a synthetic and pluralistic approach may provide the best road to future progress. (Van Gulik, 2004)

Allama Jafari does not refute the idea of a pluralistic approach to the question of consciousness, but he seems to provide a workable definition of what is meant by "consciousness" or *Agahi*, which is of pivotal role in understanding the poetry of knowledge and science in the constitution of the "intelligible paradigm" for the sustenance of self and society. According to Allama Jafari,

> it means that the human being is a living reality, and for the continuance of life he needs to exercise supervision on all possible dimensions which life may unfold. This supervision cannot be realized without a conscious approach to the question of life in all its aspects, such as interpersonal relationships, societal relationships, and the complex relations which exist between man and nature. In addition, it is of great significance to note that the quest of knowledge is not only an epiphenomenon of sociological nature in its totality. On the contrary, this quest is deeply intertwined with the essence of humanity *qua* human beings. This is not to deny the similarities between the naturalistic and intelligible paradigms in terms of desire to know, as both paradigms promote this quest. (Jafari 1387, 126)

In other words, Allama Jafari is aware that the distinction between worldviews is not of insignificant importance as both paradigms are friendly towards the question of knowledge, but what differs between the former and the latter, he says, "is the question of 'telos,' or the teleological dimension, which seems to be disregarded in the naturalistic paradigm while it has been hailed by the proponents of the intelligible frame of reference" (Jafari 1387, 126–27).

Allama Jafari, to put it differently, argues that

> science is an attempt to perform two broad tasks of (a) unearthing aspects of great varieties of unknown dimensions which may occur in the course of human interactions with the gamut of reality, and (b) operationalization of science, like building an apartment, which is an expression of architectural sciences. (Jafari 1387, 127)

To put it succinctly, these fundamental aspects of science are not denied within the parameters of the intelligible framework at all. On the contrary, these aspects are considered to be of imperative importance, but what is of great dispute between the proponents of naturalism and the primordial school of social theory is how to interpret these empirical questions in the overall context of knowledge. In other words, Allama Jafari explains,

> We do not deny these two tasks of science. On the contrary, we are attempting to clarify that, thanks to the "imperativeness of leben," these tasks need to be married with a higher form of reality that touches the domain of "ethos," which conditions us to ask about the ideal of science while being concerned about the idea and factual state of science as a human pursuit. This is another way of ask-

ing about the relation between fact and value, which has been neglected in the course of history of science based on a pretext that these twains shall not meet as they are of different ontological orders. Of course I do not buy this, and I vehemently argue that this marriage is desirably possible provided we, *qua* human beings, have achieved a sense of autonomy which is higher than previous states of release and liberty. (Jafari 1387, 126–30)

In other words, the roles of science and the essence of knowledge "are evident in the context of the intelligible paradigm as they are meant to cultivate the possibility of autonomy in the soul of the human self *qua* a divine being who can traverse the abyss of is-ness and ought-to" (Jafari, 1387, 130).

## Ontology

Inquiring about the concept of "ontology" appears like an existential search in cataloguing the scope of being. William Shakespeare, in his *Hamlet*, seems to allude to this dilemma when he states that *There are more things in heaven and earth, Horatio, than are dreamt of in your philosophy*. In other words, ontology is the study of the *categories* of things that exist or may exist in some domain. The product of such a study is a catalog of the types of things that are assumed to exist in a domain of interest *D* from the perspective of a person who uses a language *L* for the purpose of talking about *D*. The types in the ontology represent the *predicates*, *word senses*, or *concept* and *relation types* of the language *L* when used to discuss topics in the domain *D*. An uninterpreted logic, such as predicate calculus, conceptual graphs, or knowledge interchange format, is *ontologically neutral*. It imposes no constraints on the subject matter or the way the subject may be characterized. By itself, logic says nothing about anything, but the combination of logic with ontology provides a language that can express relationships about the entities in the domain of interest.

An informal ontology may be specified by a catalog of types that are either undefined or defined only by statements in a natural language. A formal ontology is specified by a collection of names for concept and relation types organized in a partial ordering by the type-subtype relation. Formal ontologies are further distinguished by the way the subtypes are distinguished from their supertypes: an *axiomatized ontology* distinguishes subtypes by axioms and definitions stated in a formal language, such as logic or some computer-oriented notation that can be translated to logic; a *prototype-based ontology* distinguishes subtypes by a comparison with a typical member or *prototype* for each subtype. Large ontologies often use a mixture of definitional methods: formal axioms and definitions are used for the terms in mathematics, physics, and engineering; and prototypes are used for plants, animals, and common household items.[4]

Although it should be confessed that Allama Jafari does not approach the question of ontology in a disciplinary fashion by isolating it in a specific manner, this does not prevent him from engaging with this question within the parameters of his own intelligible paradigm. He argues that the question of ontology is a direct quest about the quiddity of being as the only key that can unearth the reality of leben before the human self. Allama Jafari holds that "undoubtedly, it is possible to fathom the entire gamut of being solely through the prism of the intelligible paradigm, which views the scope of leben in terms of the real aspect of the world in a phenomenal sense and the ideal dimension of the world in a noumenal sense" (Jafari 1387, 130).

It seems that Allama Jafari is thinking of some kind of dialectics between mind/reality and phenomenon/noumenon, but the question is, how does he conceptualize the dialectics between "mind" and "reality," or between "phenomenon" and "noumenon"? In his view, the natural aspect of material reality consists of "visible phenomena, quantifiable as well as qualitative indices which are perceivable to our senses and minds, problematizable for scientists in laboratories, and conceptualized by different disciplines at various research centers. In other words, the world is not chimerical but a very real fact" (Jafari 1387, 130–31).

It would be a grave mistake to assume that the whole gamut of reality is reducible to *Phaenomen* without any sense of transcendence, which, indeed, is the very core of *Phaenomen* that refers to a symbolic reality of which it is an "observable occurrence." Allama Jafari holds that the world in its realness cannot be solely reduced to the phenomenal domain and that we should realize that while reality is a material fact, its simultaneous immateriality is, so to speak, not of a fictional nature. In other words, as he explains,

> if we cannot have an intelligible vision of reality, where both material and immaterial dimensions are accommodated in an intelligible fashion, we may fall into various kinds of dualism, Aristotelianism (Matter and Form), Neo-Platonism or Kantianism (*das Ding an Sich and Das Ding für Sich*) and Hegelianism, which have deprived us of an integral understanding of the world in its entirety. (Jafari 1387, 132)

The question of ontology in Jafarian social theory is neither spiritualist nor materialist. It seems to be of a primordial nature, where both the phenomenal and noumenal are of vital significance in deciphering the complexity of reality, self, world, God, and society. In other words, there are more things in heaven and earth than are dreamt of in the disciplinary paradigm of ontology, both within social theory and the philosophical systems of modernism and humanism.

## *Weltanschauung*

The question of "worldview" is one of the most contested notions in social theory and philosophy. There are many who oppose the very problematization of "worldview" in relation to the construction of sociological theories, while others insist on the decisive role of worldviews in the constitution of theories. In other words, to discuss the problem of weltanschauung is equal to bringing up fundamental issues such as anthropology, ethics, morality, religion, gnosis, science, knowledge, theology, eschatology, teleology, deontology, and so on. It is interesting to note that Allama Jafari has paid a great deal of attention to this question by distinguishing between "picturing the world" and "conceptualizing the world." In his words,

> taking snapshots of the world as it appears to us both internally and externally is one question, and to get knowledge about the world and where we are through all possible means which could equip us with a rounded view about the nature of reality and the reality of nature in all its aspects and dimensions is of totally another order and is incomparable to the aforementioned position of picturing the world of reality in a random fashion. (Jafari 1387, 132)

Further, he adds, "what we term as weltanschauung is the ability to distinguish between various dimensions of reality, such as the mathematical and aesthetical, without losing sight of the unity of being amongst the diversity which rules over the phenomenal world" (133).

This brings us to a very postmodern idea that has occupied the minds of sociologists and social theorists, who argue that the notion of objectivity entertained by modernists seems to be of a fictional nature as the human subject does play a vital role in the process of knowledge-construction. In other words, the human being *qua* an active agent is capable of building his/her own worldview, provided the self has reached the heights of consciousness, as this requires a supervising role for the "ego" in the course of life. Allama Jafari seems to argue for an objective possibility of finding knowledge as reality is not of a constructivist nature but "real." This would entail a realist approach to the question of worldview, which is of profound significance in Jafarian social theory. Allama Jafari writes, "without an objective view of the gamut of reality it would be impossible to achieve the 'grand destination of life,' which is the core of intelligible life" (Jafari 1387, 134).

## Art

Among contemporary social theorists and philosophers of Iran, Allama Jafari stands out in terms of his approach to art as an intellectual issue that needs to be theorized. It has been conceptualized by Jafari within the parameters of "intelligible life." Jafari specifically wrote a book on art titled *Aesthetics and Art in Islamic Perspective*, where he attempted to offer a foundation for the sociological study of art. He argued that art is a *weltanschauung*, a window into the world through which we can identify and explore the webs of beliefs and social contexts of artistic forms. He highlighted the traditional theoretical perspectives of the Functional, Conflict, and Interpretivist approaches to ground a framework through which to study art intelligibly, that is to say, from within the parameters of "intelligible life." He argues:

> We can talk about three broad approaches to art: a) art for art, b) art for humanity, and c) art for the intelligible life of humanity. As we are more concerned with art in the context of the intelligible life, we need to deconstruct it into two parts, namely: the question of the meaning of life and the meaningful life, which we can best conceptualize in terms of self-realization based on eternality that is only conceivable within a sacrosanct paradigm. To put it in a different way, a meaningful life is a life wherein consciousness plays a vital role by transforming the quality of the self in relation to determinism versus freedom by emphasizing the emancipative role of the human spirit in overcoming the abyss of necessity versus freedom. Thus, if we agree that art not only refers to visual and auditory artifacts, e.g., painting, sculpture, and music, but also is a *weltanschauung*, a medium to look onto the world, it could be maintained that art for humanity in the context of the intelligible life is the power to imagine reality as it is in conjunction with reality as it ought to be through a transcendental vision. (Jafari 1387, 135–36)

This is to argue, he elaborates, that "art is an existential exercise in setting free the human soul by awakening it to a higher reality where the domains of necessity and freedom have been consciously seen through" (136).

But within the hegemonic naturalist paradigm, art, Allama Jafari says, has "lost its sense of commitment by replacing 'intellect' with 'sensuality.' This has given rise to a worldview where 'consciousness,' 'liberty,' 'search for meaning' and all other lofty ideals have lost their appeal" (Jafari 1387, 136–37).

In other words, the question of art within the Jafarian paradigm is not equal to the technical usage of this term within the disciplinary sociology of art. When Allama Jafari is talking about art, he is asking about reality. In this regard, he asks,

> What is reality? Our historical epoch resonates with a single voice—What is reality? For the first time, [art] has truly become the expression of a *weltanschauung*, a "view-of-the-world," in the most literal sense of the term. The artist views the world to explain it for its real context, its truth. What is reality? (Jaffe 1964, Introduction)

Art for humanity within the parameters of the intelligible life is concerned about the nature of reality as the emancipation of the self without this realization is impossible. This is the Jafarian approach to the sociology of art in a primordial fashion which needs to be deconstructed and compared with current discourses on art in sociology, social theory and the humanities.

## Politics

Allama Jafari divides the idea of politics into two broad domains of "real" and "actual." He further provides a definition for each which enables him to put forward his own approach within the parameters of the primordial school of social theory. He argues that the concept of "politics" is one of the most controversial ideas which have been rigged both intellectually and practically. However, he says, there is a possibility to define the concept of politics "in a consciously reasonable fashion which takes into prime consideration the integral reality of the human being in a social equation. Based on this [primordial approach], we can define politics as an integral way of organizing human lives which can be conducive in achieving the noblest goals of both material and transcendental significance" (Jafari 1387, 137). This is what Allama Jafari terms a "real definition" of politics, which is distinguished from the "actual practice" of politicians, who have reduced such a lofty ideal into, as he puts it, "one of the most horrible theaters in the history of humanity by reducing the question of life in terms of human beings into an issue of life in terms of reified commodities that are entangled in the cash nexus and webs of consuming [cultures of modernity]" (137).

In other words, politics within the parameters of the "intelligible life" is an attempt to remove the obstacles before humanity that has been entangled in various forms of "reification," "alienation," "fragmentation," "commodification," and "disorientation." Allama Jafari has a very interesting way of approaching the alienating mode of modernist as well as despotic political forms by using two Persian terms: *Chiz* and *Kas*, which, respectively, mean "Some-Thing" and "Some-One" in English. In this regard, he argues that "the mission of politics is to turn some-things into some-ones and not vice versa, as we have witnessed in the course of human history that has been ruled by a naturalistic approach to existence" (Jafari 1387, 140).

This play on words is not only of semantic importance but it of ontological significance, as Allama Jafari is trying to make a vital point in relation to social organization and the human personality within the parameters of the primordial school of social theory.

## Economy

The decisive role assigned to the economic domain is undisputed by Allama Jafari. He believes that economic issues are of great importance in the constitution of the self in society. But what is disputed in the Jafarian approach in conceptualizing the problematique of economics is the manner in which naturalist thinkers have problematized two vital questions of "self-preservation" and "self-love." He argues that "those who think within the parameters of the naturalistic paradigm tend to think in an exclusive fashion, which leads ultimately in distorting the existential significance of 'self,' 'preservation' and 'love'" (Jafari 1387, 140).

Allama Jafari explains his approach to the question of economy within the intelligible paradigm in the following terms:

> The importance of love cannot be understood as long as we are under the spell of naturalism, which equates blind egotism with self-love without realizing that the idea of the self would make no sense if there is no essence and that what is supposed to be preserved are not the carnal routines of life but the essential dimensions of the human person, which we term as the "self." This is conceivable solely when we are conscious about the "eternal law of unselfishness." (Jafari 1387, 141)

He adds: "We can define economics in terms of the right of ownership, which is concomitant with the ideal of liberty. Within the paradigm of intelligible life, we can give a rounded definition of how economics should be organized, of how the right of life should be conceded to everybody" (142). And further elaborates: "It is inconceivable to have an intelligible economic system without taking into serious consideration the imperatives of truth, the other, and the mutual acceptance of self and others" (143).

Allama Jafari seems to suggest an economic system where ethics plays a vital role in the constitution of economic policies, but he is also conscious that within the contemporary world order, his approach may come across as utopian. But to those who may accuse him of escapism, Allama Jafari contends that "they need to revisit their conceptions about life as utopia is not an external domain forced on the very textures of life. On the contrary, it is life in its marvelous fashion which is not bogged down in the swamps of egotism, narcissism and a despicable sense of tutelage" (Jafari 1387, 145).

## Education and Pedagogy

Education is not only about information but also relates to the inner formation of the human subject. This is a fundamental aspect of pedagogy in the Jafarian frame of reference, which is based on the notion of "leading upward." Education within the parameters of primordial school of social theory aims at "enhancing the perceptual faculties of the human self in learning the authentic realities of life by moving gradually through the stages of 'naturalistic lifestyle' and entering, finally, into the realm of the 'intelligible life'" (Jafari 1387, 145).

In other words, the question of education or *paidagōgeō* within Jafarian discourse is not separated from Allama Jafari's anthropological conception, which is founded on a particular ontology where the realms of being are conceptualized in an integral fashion. This is to argue that Allama Jafari assigns a significant role for education in the constitution of the self and society, and in transforming the parameters of human existence from a naturalistic paradigm into an intelligible frame of reference. He explains that "an intelligible educational approach is not solely concerned with the sensual or mental dimensions of the human self, which may be based upon imparting knowledge or transmitting information without taking into consideration the normative significance of reality in the constitution of the human self" (Jafari 1387, 146).

Allama Jafari thus suggests that education needs to engage the whole of the human being if we believe in the possibility of redemption, which is one of the salient signs of the "intelligible life."

## NOTES

1. Seyed Jalal Al-e-Ahmad (1923–1969) was a prominent Iranian writer, thinker, and social and political critic. Although he lived a short life, he was a prolific writer. He wrote the following:

Novels and Novellas

- *The School Principal*
- *By the Pen*
- *The Tale of Beehives*
- *The Cursing of the Land*
- *A Stone upon a Grave*

Short Stories

- "The Setar"
- "Of Our Suffering"
- "Someone Else's Child"
- "Pink Nail Polish"
- "The Chinese Flower Pot"
- "The Treasure"
- "The Postman"
- "The Pilgrimage"
- "Sin"

Critical Essays

- "Seven Essays"
- "Hurried Investigations"
- "Plagued by the West" (Westoxification)

Monographs (as an anthropologist with a sociological approach, Jalal traveled to far-off, usually poor, regions of Iran and tried to document the life, culture, and problems of the people living there; some of these monographs are listed below)

- "Owrazan"
- "The People of Block-e-Zahra"
- "Kharg Island, the Unique Pearl of the Persian Gulf"

Travelogues

- *A Straw in Mecca*
- *A Journey to Russia*
- *A Journey to Europe*
- *The Land of Azrael*
- *A Journey to America*

Translations
- *The Gambler* by Fyodor Dostoyevsky
- *L'Etranger* by Albert Camus
- *Les Mains Sales* by Jean-Paul Sartre
- *Return from the U.S.S.R.* by André Gide
- *Rhinoceros* by Eugène Ionesco

2. This part of the discussion is based on my private debate with Dr. Rohit Barot from Bristol University, who has helped me to realize the shortcomings of rationalization theory from a Hindu perspective.

3. By this term, I refer to its pristine meaning, which is based on the ability of the human self to exercise "autonomy" and choose the path of self-realization.

4. See the following link: http://www.jfsowa.com/ontology/.

# Epilogue

## UNIVERSALIZING EUROPE PROVINCIALIZING EUROPE?

In a recent book, Georg Stauth and Marcus Otto (2008) analysed the Mediterranean, la méditerranée, as the space of negative projection of European modernity. If we try to think the Mediterranean as the "Other" of the identity of the European subject constituting this identity and thought of as its prehistory, we understand that the principles of binary opposition dominating the constitution of European universalist ideas (subject/object, ratio/eros, rationality/irrationality, general/singular, etc.) are based on a binary opposition: occidental/oriental. These oppositions are reproduced by constantly referring to them, recognising, naturalising, reifying. In other words, the West finds its putative unity through statements about itself and its differences in a discursive formation called "the-West-and-the Rest," by Stuart Hall. This discursive configuration influences the configuration of disciplines in the humanities. Naoki Sakai analysed this configuration in an excellent way. So a lengthy quote may be justified:[1]

> The unity of the West seems to bestow a sense of coherence upon the configuration of disciplines in the humanities. It serves to mark a distinction between the areas and peoples that can be objects of ethnic and area and those that cannot. People in the West ordinarily do not receive the attribute "ethnic," because, supposedly, they are not to be defined in terms of their status as an object of study: before being studied, known, and recognised, they are expected to take an active attitude in studying, knowing and recognising. Instead of being passively inspected, classified, compared, and analysed, they are supposed to engage in applying their own means of inspection, classification, comparison, and analysis to some object, which might well be themselves. . . . In short in this epistemic transaction, the West insists on being determined in terms not of

its characteristics as an object of knowledge but rather of its subjective faculties and productivity.

Accordingly, we could discern two radical different ways for people to relate themselves to the production of knowledge in the humanities. The group of people whose regional, civilizational, national, or ethnic identity constitutes the objective legitimacy of the discipline would participate within that discipline in the production of knowledge, primarily as suppliers of raw data and factual information. They neither need to engage in the application of a classificatory system nor of the evaluative methods in the processing of such data, nor the preparation of an epistemic framework through which the data are appropriated into a general interpretive narrative. . . .

On the other hand, there is another sort of people, who seek to know about humanity and human nature, but who would never be content to be suppliers of information. For them, knowing is an essential part of their being, so that their way of life will be affected as their relationship to knowledge-production changes. They necessarily engage in the collection, evaluation, comparison, or analysis of raw data, but, more importantly, they are continually involved in the critical review of the existing means of knowing and the invention of new means. . . . The project of changing and creating the means of knowing is sometimes called "theory", and it is taken to be a distinguishing mark or even mission of the West. In this sense "theory" is presumably the essence of Western humanity. (Sakai 2001, 197–98)

This process of producing European superiority via specific divisions in the disciplines of humanities and the material preconditions of this superiority are in the process of being undermined. The participation of an increasing number of non-Westerners, non-Europeans, non-Americans in the creation and change of knowledge destroy the very fundament of this exclusively Western humanity. Pushed ahead by global modernization, cultural, political, and economic interchange between different regions brought different forms of power and knowledge into more intense interaction, thus forcing Western academia to begin to change. It's the beginning we are witnessing, not a thorough reconfiguration of Western thought.

The appearance of Islam in the 1970s on the political landscape, on the culturescape, to adopt Appudaraian ways of speaking, on the landscape of discourse in general and specifically in European (North American, Australian etc.) societies, in the streets, and in the media is one of the most important processes undermining European universalist domination, and it is causing direct reactions: anti-Islamic, Islamophobic, but also the explorations of new approaches to European universality. One of the best known—and often misunderstood—examples may be the experience of Michel Foucault 1978/79 in Iran; others are the highly diverse postcolonial and "post-postcolonial"

(Loomba 2006) critique of European universalism or the critique of Eurocentric constructions of world history.

We will not have to look into thousands of anti-Islamic books and texts of a pure eurocentric kind[2] to illustrate the first aspect, but the second aspect is much more interesting. André Gunder Frank (2005) describes the different approaches trying to deconstruct former eurocentric theories. Theories questioning the idea of the oriental world constructed by Europeans, theories negating the unique role of the Western way of development, comparative research on the differences between "western" and "eastern" societies and world system theories still thinking of Europe as the centre of the world at all. We won't discuss Frank's new approach of a holistic theory of development, but we'll focus on one idea not mentioned by Frank: the integration of European and non-European systems of thought, as Seyed Javad Miri put it: "Cartesian" and "Sadraian" thought. Or, as Marshall G. Hodgson (1993) put it, we have to acknowledge that a purely Western-oriented idea of history will cause immense mischief all over the world if not corrected by alternative points of view.

The integration of Islamic discourses into European ones, however, remains very spurious. We may think of the German Marxist philosopher Ernst Bloch (1985) who wrote in 1952 on Avicenna and the Aristotelian left trying to construct the tradition of Ibn Sina, Ibn Rushd et al. as part of the prehistory (sic!) of European materialist thought, generously admitting that there may be a Muslim way to European modernity and accepting the influence of this tradition on European philosophers and theologians.[3] This study may be part of the more interesting part of literature on Islam in Europe, but it is still a case of constructing Islam as subaltern to European modernities.

One more recent example is a short treatise of the Italian philosopher Girogio Agamben called "Bartleby or On Contingency" (1989). Agamben integrates—starting from Aristoteles—thoughts of Avicenna, Ibn 'Arabi, and Shihab al-Din al-Suhrawardi into one continuous discourse without subordinating the Islamic writers into a European-dominated discourse, and needless to emphasize, this change of orientation points to a promising openness of thought rarely found in contemporary European discourses.

We might say that there are ways to include Islamic and other thoughts into European discourses and benefit from these thoughts. But as a fact, we have to admit that there is little knowledge of advanced Islamic thought in Europe, and one important task is to raise the consciousness of the importance of knowing this part of modernity. This is a task not only for Europeans but also for non-Europeans. So we are facing a double challenge: to change the Eurocentric construction of knowledge (in the humanities and natural sciences) and to integrate Islamic, Asian, African, and South and Middle American knowledge with a de-Europeanized knowledge into a new system of knowledge characterized by non-homogenized approaches.

If we are to accept the idea of Immanuel Wallerstein that we are at the end of a long era he called "the era of European universalism," then we can expect to be at the beginning of an era of a "diversity of universalisms" or of networks of universalisms. The universalizing of European universalism is the only way to overcome the alternative: a hierarchical world ruled by inequality, racism, and sexism but claiming to be ruled by universal values exclusively European-American (Wallerstein 2007, 96–97).

The evolving globality of theory demands a new definition of the humanities as a theory that is not the sole possession of European humanity, "a form of theorizing that is attentive to the transcultural dissemination and global traces within theoretical knowledge produced in geopolitical locations and which explores how theories are themselves transformed by their practical effects when they are performed in other sites" (Sakai 2001, 214).

So coming back to specific Islamic topics: Engaging the post-Avicennan and post-Suhrawardian thought of Iran and India, especially the "School of Isfahan," is not only a distinct operation of a circle of scholars inspired by the example of Henri Corbin (Lutrand 2004) and interested in transcendental philosophy but also an important task for other disciplines in the humanities, e.g., the social sciences. Even if we think of the unity of knowledge including sciences to be found in the works of Shihab al-din al-Suhrawardi, a contribution to philosophy of science may be interesting.

Entering into a realistic discussion of what can be expected of the experience of hybridization of social sciences and humanities demands a thorough knowledge of systems of thought other than the European ones.

The work of Seyed Javad Miri on Allama Jafari is one of the most interesting contributions to the process of constructing new networks of universalisms. His presentation of the multidimensional thought of Allama Jafari will inspire novel attempts of conceptualizing true universal theories.

We should think in the context of Dipesh Chakrabarty's idea of provincializing Europe (Chakrabarty 2002), understanding modernity as a contested field where the struggle for true universalism is fought. Then we will be able to join theoreticians like Seyed Javad Miri and to understand the role of thinkers like Avicenna, as-Suhrawardi, Mulla Sadra, and, more recently, Allama Jafari.

Rüdiger Lohlker
Professur für Orientalistik an der
Philologisch-Kulturwissenschaftlichen Fakultät
Vienna, Austria

## NOTES

1. This analysis has to be supplemented by an intersectional discussion of gender-ized knowledge. This cannot be done here.
2. We have to think of the first bestsellers on the European book market: anti-Muslim/Osmanic pamphlets.
3. A fact sometimes denied today, cf. Gouguenheim 2008.


## BIBLIOGRAPHY TO EPILOGUE

Agamben, G. 1998. *Bartleby oder die Kontingenz gefolgt von Die absolute Imma-nenz*. Berlin: Merve.
Bloch, E. 1985. "Avicenna und die Aristotelische Linke." In *Das Materialismuspro-blem, seine Geschichte und Substanz*. Frankfurt a.M.: Suhrkamp.
Chakrabarty, D. 2002. "Europa provinzialisieren. Postkolonialität und die Kritik der Geschichte." In *Jenseits des Eurozentrismus. Postkoloniale Perspektiven in den Geschichts- und Kulturwissenschaften*, ed. Conrad/S. Randeria. Frankfurt/New York: Campus Verlag.
Frank, A. G. 2005. *Orientierung im Weltsystem*. Wien: Promedia.
Gouguenheim, S. 2008. *Aristote au Mont Sain-Michel. Les racines grecques de l'Europe chrétienne*. Paris: Editions du Seuil.
Hodgson, M. G. 1993. *Rethinking World History*, ed. E. Burke III. Cambridge: Cam-bridge University Press.
Loomba, A., ed. 2006. *Postcolonial Studies and Beyond*. Durham, NC: Duke Uni-versity Press.
Lutrand, M.-C. 2004. *La rencontre de l'Orient et de l'Occident: Henry Corbin et Al-lameh Tabatabai*. Toulouse: Institut de Science et de Theologie des Religions.
Sakai, N. 2001. "Dislocation of the West and the Status of the Humanities." In *Unpacking Europe. Towards a Critical Reading*, ed. S. Hassan and I. Dadi. Rot-terdam: Museum Boijmans Van Beuningen, S.196–215.
Stauth, G., and M. Otto. 2008. *Méditerranée: Skizzen zu Mittelmeer, Islam und Theo-rie der Moderne*. Berlin: Kadmos.
Wallerstein, I. 2007. *Die Barbarei der anderen. Europäischer Universalismus*. Ber-lin: Wagenbach.

# Sources

Allport, G. W. 1955. *Becoming: Basic Considerations for a Psychology of Personality*. New Haven, CT. Yale University Press.

Assagioli, R. 1965. *Psychosynthesis*. New York: Hobbs, Dorman.

Barnes, Barry, and David Bloor. 1982. "Relativism, Rationalism and the Sociology of Knowledge." In *Rationality and Relativism*, ed. Martin Hollis and Steven Lukes. Oxford: Basil Blackwell, 1982.

Bolen, J. S. 1984. *Goddesses in Every Woman*. New York: Harper & Row.

Bridges, W. 2004. *Transitions: Making Sense of Life's Changes*. New York: De Capo Press.

Buber, M. 1978. *I and Thou*. Riverside, NJ: Macmillan.

Bugental, J. F. T. 1965. *The Search for Existential Identity*. New York: Holt, Rinehart and Winston.

Bugental, J. F. T. 1992. *The Art of Psychotherapy*. New York: W. W. Norton.

Camus, A. 1954. *The Rebel*. New York: A. A. Knopf.

Capra, F. 1982. *The Turning Point*. New York: Bantam.

Cox, H. 1968. *The Secular City: Secularization and Urbanization in Theological Perspective*. Harmondsworth: Penguin.

Durkheim, Emile. 1950 [1895]. *The Rules of Sociological Method*. Trans. S. A. Solovay and J. H. Mueller. New York: The Free Press.

———. 1951 [1897]. *Suicide: A Study in Sociology*. Trans. J. A. Spaulding and G. Simpson. New York: The Free Press.

———. 1954 [1912]. *The Elementary Forms of the Religious Life*. Trans. by J. W. Swain. New York: The Free Press.

———. 1953. *Sociology and Philosophy*. New York: The Free Press.

———. 1956. *Education and Sociology*. Trans. S. D. Fox. New York: The Free Press.

———. 1960 [1893]. *The Division of Labor in Society*. Translated by George Simpson. New York: The Free Press.

———. 1961. *Moral Education: A Study in the Theory and Application of the Sociology of Education.* Translated by E. K. Wilson and H. Schnurer. New York: The Free Press.

Ellis, A. 1973. *Humanistic Psychology: The Rational-Emotive Approach.* New York: Julian Press.

Ferguson, M. 1980. *The Aquarian Conspiracy.* Los Angeles: Jeremy P. Tarcher.

Flanagan, Owen. 1995. "Consciousness." In *The Oxford Companion to Philosophy*, ed. Ted Honderich. Oxford: University of Oxford Press, 1995.

Frankl, V. 1984. *Man's Search for Meaning.* New York: Pocket Books.

Fromm, E. 1989. *The Art of Loving.* New York: Harper & Row.

Gendlin, E. 1981. *Focusing.* New York: Bantam.

Georgi, A. 1970. *Psychology as a Human Science.* New York: Harper & Row.

Gibb, J. 1978. *Trust.* Los Angeles: Guild of Tutors Press.

Grof, Stanislav. 1993. *The Holotropic Mind: The Three Levels of Human Consciousness and How They Shape Our Mind.* San Francisco: Harper SanFrancisco, 1993.

———. 1985. *Beyond the Brain: Birth, Death, and Transcendence in Psychotherapy.* Albany, NY: SUNY Press.

———. 1988. *The Adventure of Self-Discovery.* Albany, NY: SUNY Press.

Harris, Marvin. 2000. *The Rise of Anthropological Theory.* Lanham, MD: AltaMira Press.

Heidegger, M. 1962. *Being and Time.* New York: Harper & Row.

Hillman, J. 1975. *Revisioning Psychology.* New York: Harper & Row.

———. 1995. *Kinds of Power.* New York: Doubleday.

Houston, J. 1982. *The Possible Human.* Los Angeles: Jeremy P. Tarcher.

Jafari, M. T. 1334. *The Relationship between Man and the Universe.* Tehran: Akhundi Publishing House.

———. 1385. *Aesthetics and Art in Islamic Perspective.* Tehran: Center for Allama Jafari Studies.

———. 1386. *Message of Wisdom.* Tehran: Center for Allama Jafari Studies.

———. 1387. *Intelligible Life.* Tehran: Center for Allama Jafari Studies.

———. 2002. *The Conscience.* Tehran: Center for Allama Jafari Studies.

James, W. 1901–02/1977. *The Varieties of Religious Experience.* Fountain Books.

Jourard, S. 1964. *The Transparent Self.* Princeton, NJ: Van Nostrand.

Jung, C. G. 1953–79. *The Collected Works of C. G. Jung.* Translated by R.F.C. Hull. Princeton, NJ: Princeton University Press.

———. 1989. *Memories, Dreams, Reflections.* New York: Random House.

Jung, C. G., ed. 1964. *Man and His Symbols.* Garden City, NY: Doubleday & Company.

Kelly, Sean. 1988. "Hegel and Morin: The Science of Wisdom and the Wisdom of the New Science." *The Owl of Minerva: Biannual Journal of the Hegel Society of America* 20(1): 1–67.

———. 1993. *Individuation and the Absolute: Hegel, Jung, and the Path Toward Wholeness.* Mahwah, NJ: Paulist Press.

———. 1998. "Revisioning the Mandala of Consciousness." In *Ken Wilber in Dialogue: Conversations with Leading Transpersonal Thinkers*, ed. Donald Rothberg and Sean Kelly. Wheaton, IL: Quest Books.

———. 2009. "Transpersonal Psychology and the Paradigm of Complexity." Accessed at: http://www.purifymind.com/TranspersonalPsy.htm.

Laing, R. D. 1965. *The Divided Self.* New York: Penguin.

Lowry, R., ed. 1979. *The Journals of A. H. Maslow.* Monterey, CA: Brooks/Cole.

Leydesdorff, L. 2002. "May There Be A 'Socionomy' Beyond 'Sociology'?" *SCI-POLICY—The Journal of Science and Health Policy* 2(1). Accessed at http://home .att.net/~Scipolicy/index.htm.

Maslow, A. H. 1954. *Motivation and Personality.* New York: Harper & Brothers.

———. 1968. *Toward a Psychology of Being.* 2d ed. Princeton, NJ: Van Nostrand.

———. 1976. *The Farther Reaches of Human Nature.* New York: Penguin.

May, R. 1950. *The Meaning of Anxiety.* New York: Ronald Press.

———. 1983. *The Discovery of Being.* New York: W. W. Norton.

———. 1984. *The Courage to Create.* New York: Bantam.

Murphy, M. 1992. *The Future of the Body.* Los Angeles: J. P. Tarcher.

Moore, T. 1993. *The Care of the Soul.* New York: HarperCollins.

Morin, Edgar. 1977. *La Methode I: La Nature de la Nature.* Paris: Editions du Seuil. This volume has been somewhat literally translated by J. L. Roland Belanger, *Method: Toward a Study of Human Nature: Vol. I. The Nature of Nature.* New York: Peter Lang Publishing Inc., 1992.

———. 1980. *La Methode II: La Vie de la Vie.* Paris: Editions du Seuil

———. 1986. *La Methode III, i: La Connaissance de la Connaissance.* Paris: Editions du Seuil.

———. 1981. *Pour Sortir du XXe Siecle.* Paris: Fernand Nathan.

———. 1982. *Science avec Conscience.* Paris: Fayard.

Morin, Edgar (with Anne Brigitte Kern). 1998. *Homeland Earth: A Manifesto for the New Millennium.* Translated by S. M. Kelly and R. Lapointe. Kreskill, NJ: Hampton Press.

Moustakas, C. 1961. *Loneliness.* Englewood Cliffs, NJ: Prentice-Hall.

———. 1994. *Existential Psychotherapy and the Interpretation of Dreams.* Northvale, NJ: J. Aronson.

Myers, Frederic. 1903/1954. *Human Personality and Its Survival of Bodily Death.* 2 vols. Longmans, Green, & Co.

Neumann, E. 1955. *The Great Mother.* New York: Pantheon.

Ortega y Gasset, J. 1957. *Man and People.* New York: W. W. Norton.

Perls, F. 1973. *The Gestalt Approach and Eyewitness to Therapy.* Palo Alto, CA: Science & Behavior Books.

Polkinghorne, D. E. 1988. *Narrative Knowing and the Human Sciences.* Albany, NY: SUNY Press.

Reich, W. 1949. *Character Analysis.* New York: Orgone Institute Press.

———. 1973. *Function of the Orgasm.* New York: Farrar, Straus and Giroux.

Ricoeur, P. 1970. *Freud and Philosophy.* New Haven, CT: Yale University Press.

Rogers, C. R. 1951. *Client-Centered Therapy.* Boston: Houghton Mifflin.

———. 1972. *On Becoming a Person.* Boston: Houghton Mifflin.

———. 1980. *A Way of Being.* Boston: Houghton Mifflin.

Romanyshyn, R. 1989. *Technology as Symptom and Dream.* London & New York: Routledge.

Roszak, T., A. K. Kanner, and M. E. Gomes, M. E., ed. 1955. *Ecopsychology.* San Francisco: Sierra Club.

Sardello, R. 1992. *Facing the World with Soul.* New York: Harper Perennial.

Sartre, J.-P. 1956. *Being and Nothingness.* New York: Philosophical Library.

Satir, V. 1972. *People-Making.* Palo Alto, CA: Science & Behavior Books.

Schutz, W. C. 1967. *Joy.* New York: Grove Press.

Strasser, S. 1963. *Phenomenology and the Human Science.* Pittsburgh, PA: Duquesne University Press.

Thoreau, H. D. 1922. *Walden.* Library of America.

Tillich, P. 1932. *The Courage To Be.* New Haven, CT: Yale University Press.

Valle, R. J., and M. King, eds. 1978. *Existential-Phenomenological Alternatives for Psychology.* New York: Oxford University Press.

Van den Berg, J. H. 1961. *The Changing Nature of Man.* New York: W. W. Norton and Company.

Van Dusen, W. 1976. *The Natural Depth in Man.* New York: Harper & Row.

Van Gulik, Robert. 2004. *Consciousness.* Accessed at: http://plato.stanford.edu/entries/consciousness/.

Wallerstein, Immanuel. 2003. "Anthropology, Sociology, and Other Dubious Disciplines." *Current Anthropology* 44:453–66.

Walsh, R., and F. Vaughn, eds. 1980. *Beyond Ego: Transpersonal Dimensions in Psychology.* Los Angeles: Jeremy P. Tarcher, Inc.

———. 1993. *Paths Beyond Ego: Transpersonal Dimensions of Psychology.* Los Angeles: J. P. Tarcher/Perigee.

Watts, A. 1975. *Psychotherapy East and West.* New York: Random House.

Wheelis, A. 1958. *The Quest for Identity.* New York: W. W. Norton.

Wilber, Ken. 1977. *No Boundary.* Boston: New Science Library/Shambala.

———. 1981. *Up from Eden.* New York: Anchor.

———. 1983. *Eye to Eye: The Quest for the New Paradigm.* Anchor Books.

———. 1995. *Sex, Ecology, Spirituality: The Spirit of Evolution.* Boston: Shambala.

———. 1997. "An Integral Theory of Consciousness." *Journal of Consciousness Studies* 4(1): 71–92.

Wilson, C. 1961. *The Outsider.* Boston: Houghton Mifflin.

Yalom, I. 1980. *Existential Psychotherapy.* New York: Basic Books.